The
Iona Community
Worship Book

The Abbey Services of
the Iona Community

This Revised Edition 1991
Second Impression 1992

The Abbey, Iona, Argyll PA76 6SN
Tel. 06817-404

Camas Adventure Camp, Bunessan, Mull PA67 6DX
Tel. 06817-367 (Booking enquiries Tel. 06817-404)

Community House, Pearce Institute, Govan Glasgow G51 3UU
Tel. 041-445-4561

Peace House, The Old Manse, Greenloaning, Perthshire FK15 0NB
Tel. 0786-88490

Centrepeace, 143 Stockwell Street, Glasgow G1 4LR
Tel. 041-552-8357

The MacLeod Centre, Iona, Argyll PA76 6SN
Tel. 06817-404

®TM

The Wild Goose is a Celtic symbol of the Holy Spirit
It serves as the Trademark of Wild Goose Publications

WILD GOOSE PUBLICATIONS
The Publishing Division of The Iona Community

Pearce Institute, 840 Govan Road, Glasgow G51 3UU
Tel. 041-445-4561   Fax. 041-445-4295

Printed in Great Britain by
BPCC Hazell Books, Paulton and Aylesbury

CONTENTS

PREFACE

This revised edition of *The Iona Community Worship Book* concentrates exclusively on services used in Iona Abbey on a frequent basis. Some of the liturgies which appeared in the previous edition, together with some other worship material which has been used from time to time on Iona, may be obtained on request to the *Wild Goose Resource Group* at the Pearce Institute in Glasgow. Similarly the chants and songs of the Community are available in the three volumes of *Wild Goose Songs*, available from *Wild Goose Publications* at the same address.

The changes that have been made to liturgies reflect the continuing growth and development of life and worship at the Abbey, and have been shaped and contributed to by the resident group and by visiting members and friends of the Community from around the world. As well as changes to existing liturgies there is now included a service of prayer for justice and peace and a creation liturgy for possible use on Monday and Wednesday evenings respectively. In addition to the regular morning and evening services, a celtic liturgy and a new simple evening liturgy have been included along with the other alternative services. Many of the services now have appendices at the back of the book to provide specifically related worship resources and recommendations. Also there is now an appendix of inclusive language Psalms for use primarily in the morning service.

Although the principal purpose of this book is for use in the Abbey Church, it is hoped that the services and resources will be well used and adapted for use elsewhere. Our prayer is that this publication will be a contribution to the worship of God both within the church and within our common life together, and that similarly for the many who will take this book away, it will give voice to people's prayers for the world and their celebration of Christ in community.

Philip Newell
Iona Abbey
Advent, 1990

THE IONA COMMUNITY

The Iona Community is an ecumenical community of men and women, seeking new ways of living the Gospel in today's world.

The Community was founded in 1938 by the Rev. George MacLeod, the late Very Rev. Lord MacLeod of Fuinary, to be a sign of the rebuilding of the common life of the Church in the world, and to break down the barriers between prayer and politics, between the religious and the ordinary. The task around which the Community first gathered was the restoration of the ruined monastic buildings of the Abbey, the Cathedral church having already been restored under the Trustees of the Cathedral earlier in the century. An exciting recent development has been the building of the nearby MacLeod Centre, a centre for reconciliation with a special commitment to young people, and facilities for the disabled. In addition to the two centres on Iona, the Community also runs Camas, a summer camp for young people on the nearby Island of Mull.

The Community is made up at present of approximately 200 members, 900 associates, and 2000 friends. The members are men and women, lay and ordained, working in many different jobs, and coming from many countries. Since 1952 the Community has come under the auspices of the Church of Scotland. Its membership however has always been open to members of other Christian denominations, and it has always welcomed to its centres on Iona and Mull people of all traditions and faiths, or of none.

Members of the Community live in varied locations throughout the United Kingdom and abroad, and renew their commitment to the Community on a yearly basis. They are bound together by a five-fold rule of prayer and Bible study, meeting together, accountability on the use of their time and money, and working for justice and peace. The focus of the Community's work lies in the areas of ecumenical activity, work with the poor and the exploited, the struggle for justice, peace and the integrity of creation, action in relation to racism and inter-faith concerns, work with young people, and the rediscovery of spirituality for today. These concerns are reflected in the community life which all, both staff and guests, share week by week in the Community centres on the islands.

The Community maintains a resident group on Iona, to welcome the more than 100,000 visitors who come to the island each year. Between March and December the group shares its common life of work, worship and recreation with hundreds of guests, who come from all over the world to stay at one or other of the centres, usually for a week at a time. They are also joined by many voluntary staff, who come to serve the Community and share in the common life, usually for a seven week period, but sometimes for longer.

The mainland work of the Community is co-ordinated from Community House at Govan in Glasgow, where the Leader of the Community is based, together with administrative staff, The Wild Goose Worship/Resource Group and Youth Development Worker. The Community has its own magazine, *The Coracle*, its own book and craft shop (with mail-order section) in the Abbey, and its own publishing label, *Wild Goose Publications*. It shares in the work of "Centrepeace", a peace and justice resource centre and shop in Glasgow, and helps to employ a Justice and Peace Worker based in "Peace House", a residential peace centre near Stirling.

If you would like to know more about the Community, or about staying or working with the Community on Iona or Mull, please ask at the Abbey Office, or write to Community House in Glasgow: The Iona Community, Community House, Pearce Institute, 840 Govan Road, Glasgow G51 3UU.

CONCERNING WORSHIP

The services in this book reflect important aspects of what the Iona Community believes about worship.

We owe our very existence as a Community to the central Gospel conviction that worship is all that we are and all that we do. Either everything we do is an offering to God, or nothing. We may not pick and choose.

Our whole life, we believe, is a search for wholeness. We desire to be fully human, with no division into the 'sacred' and the 'secular'. We desire to be fully present to God, who is fully present to us, whether in our neighbour or in the political and social activity of the world around us, whether in the fields of culture or of economics, and whether in prayer and praise together or in the very centre and soul of our being.

Of ourselves we cannot make this happen. We cannot make ourselves whole any more than we can make ourselves happy or good. But we do believe that by grace we are to structure our lives, both individually and together, in obedience to the vision that God has given us of what wholeness is like, primarily through the life, death and resurrection of Jesus Christ.

So, on Iona, we are committed to the belief that worship is everything we do, both inside and outside the church. We begin each day with prayer together, common prayer, for we are a community, given to each other by God. In the morning service we do not end with a benediction, but simply with responses that prepare us to go straight out to the life of the world, there to continue worship in the context of our work. In the evening we come together again for common prayer, but we do not begin the service with a call to worship, for we have been at worship all day long. And only in the evening service do we have a final benediction at the close of the day.

In this symbolic way we try to express our conviction that the whole of our day is all of a piece, bracketed with common prayer, but continuing throughout every action of work and common life and recreation as one liturgy, one work of service offered to God.

On Iona, our common life is fed from many sources. The past is all

7

around us. We are the inheritors of the Celtic tradition, with its deep sense of Jesus as the head of all, and of God's glory in all of creation. So we use prayers from the Celtic Church for welcome, for work, and in expressing the needs of the world. We are the inheritors of the Benedictine tradition, with its conviction that 'to work is to pray', its commitment to hospitality, and its sense of order, all reflected in our services and our lifestyle. And we are the inheritors of the tradition of the Reformers, with their evangelical zeal, their call to commitment, and their deep understanding of the continuing challenge to every generation to find 'new ways to touch the hearts of all'. All this, we hope you will find in how we pray and work on Iona.

Because we are an ecumenical community, we also draw on many modern Christian traditions in our services. This is a great privilege for us, and something we value very highly. It also reminds us that our life and our services here are no 'hole in the corner' affair. All we are and all we do, our work and our prayer, is part of the ongoing prayer and work of the whole Church in heaven and on earth: we are part of the one communion of saints.

A time on Iona often changes people. God has clearly used this place very powerfully over the centuries. The Iona Community does not believe that we are brought here to be changed into 'religious' people, but rather to be made more fully human. Our common life, including our services, is directed to that end.

In the words of the German martyr, Dietrich Bonhoeffer, we believe that 'the Christian is not a religious person, but simply a human being, as Jesus was a human being, profoundly this-worldly, characterised by discipline, and the constant knowledge of death and resurrection'.

THE MORNING SERVICE

Opening Responses

Leader: The world belongs to God,

ALL: THE EARTH AND ALL ITS PEOPLE.

Leader: How good and how lovely it is

ALL: TO LIVE TOGETHER IN UNITY.

Leader: Love and faith come together,

ALL: JUSTICE AND PEACE JOIN HANDS.

Leader: If the Lord's disciples keep silent

ALL: THESE STONES WOULD SHOUT ALOUD.

Leader: Open our lips, O God

ALL: AND OUR MOUTHS SHALL PROCLAIM YOUR PRAISE.

Morning Hymn

Monday   **'God's Graceful Moment'**

Morning opens wide before us
Like a door into the light.
Just beyond, the day lies waiting
Ready to throw off the night,
And we stand upon its threshold
Poised to turn and take its flight.

Now the earth in all its glory
Springs to meet the rising sun,
Warms to all who walk upon it,
Cradling all that will be done,
All our labour, all our loving
Mingle and become as one.

We receive God's graceful moment,
While the day is fresh and still,
Ours to choose how we will greet it,
Ours to make it what we will.
Here is given perfect freedom,
Every hope in love to fulfil.

As we take the first step together,
Passing through the door of the day,
May the love of Christ the Creator
Give us peace in all that we say,
Heart for all that lies before us,
Grace to guide us on our way.

OR   **'Christ is Alive'**

Christ is alive, let Christians sing.
His cross stands empty to the sky.
Let streets and homes with praises ring.
His love in death shall never die.

Christ is alive, no longer bound
To distant years in Palestine.
He comes to claim the here and now
And dwell in every place and time.

Not throned afar, remotely high,
Untouched, unmoved by human pains,
But daily, in the midst of life,
Our Saviour in his mercy reigns.

In every insult, rift and war
Where colour, scorn or wealth divide,
He suffers still, yet loves the more
And lives, though ever crucified.

Christ is alive, and comes to bring
Good news to this and every age,
Till earth and all creation ring
With joy, with justice, love and praise.

Tuesday   **'Today I Awake'**

1. Today I awake
   And God is before me.
   At night, as I dreamt,
   He summoned the day;
   For God never sleeps
   But patterns the morning
   With slithers of gold
   Or glory in grey.

2. Today I arise
   And Christ is beside me.
   He walked through the dark
   To scatter new light.
   Yes, Christ is alive,
   And beckons his people
   To hope and to heal,
   Resist and invite.

3. Today I affirm
   The Spirit within me
   At worship and work,
   In struggle and rest.
   The Spirit inspires
   All life which is changing
   From fearing to faith,
   From broken to blest.

4. Today I enjoy
   The Trinity round me,
   Above and beneath,
   Before and behind;
   The Maker, the Son,
   The Spirit together –
   They called me to life
   And call me their friend.

OR   **'Tell out my Soul'**

Tell out, my soul, the greatness of the Lord!
Unnumbered blessings give my spirit voice;
Tender to me the promise of his word;
In God my Saviour shall my heart rejoice.

Tell out, my soul, the greatness of his name!
Make known his might, the deeds his arm has done;
His mercy sure, from age to age the same;
His holy name — the Lord, the mighty one.

Tell out, my soul, the greatness of his might!
Powers and dominions lay their glory by.
Proud hearts and stubborn wills are put to flight,
The hungry fed, the humble lifted high.

Tell out, my soul, the glories of his word!
Firm is his promise and his mercies sure.
Tell out, my soul, the greatness of the Lord
To children's children and for ever more!

Wednesday   **'Oh the Life of the World'**

Oh the life of the world is a joy and a treasure,
Unfolding in beauty the green-growing tree,
The changing of seasons in mountain and valley
The stars and the bright restless sea.

Oh the life of the world is a fountain of goodness
Overflowing in labour and passion and pain,
In the sound of the city and the silence of wisdom
In the birth of a child once again.

Oh the life of the world is the source of our healing.
It rises in laughter and wells up in song;
It springs from the care of the poor and the broken
And refreshes where justice is strong.

So give thanks for the life and give love to the maker
And rejoice in the gift of the bright risen Son.
And walk in the peace and the power of the Spirit
Till the days of our living are done.

OR   **'New Every Morning'**

New every morning is the love
Our wakening and uprising prove,
Through sleep and darkness safely brought,
Restored to life, and power, and thought.

New mercies, each returning day,
Hover around us while we pray;
New perils past, new sins forgiven,
New thoughts of God, new hopes of heaven.

The trivial round, the common task,
Will furnish all we ought to ask;
Room to deny ourselves, a road
To bring us daily nearer God.

Thursday　　　　　　　**'Enemy Of Apathy'**

She sits like a bird, brooding on the waters,
Hovering on the chaos of the world's first day;
She sighs and she sings, mothering creation,
Waiting to give birth to all the Word will say.

She wings over earth, resting where she wishes,
Lighting close at hand or soaring through the skies;
She nests in the womb, welcoming each wonder,
Nourishing potential hidden to our eyes.

She dances in fire, startling her spectators,
Waking tongues of ecstasy where dumbness reigned;
She weans and inspires all whose hearts are open,
Nor can she be captured, silenced or restrained.

For she is the Spirit, one with God in essence,
Gifted by the Saviour in eternal love;
She is the key opening the scriptures,
Enemy of apathy and heavenly dove.

OR　　　　　　　　　**'O Lord of Life'**

O Lord of life, your quickening voice
Awakes my morning song.
In gladsome words I would rejoice
That I to you belong.

I see your light, I feel your wind;
The world, it is your word;
Whatever wakes my heart and mind
Your presence is, my Lord.

Within my heart speak, Lord, speak on,
My heart alive to keep,
Till comes the night, and, labour done,
In you I fall asleep.

Friday　　　　　　　**'Dance and Sing'**

Chorus:　　DANCE AND SING, ALL THE EARTH,
　　　　　　GRACIOUS IS THE HAND THAT TENDS YOU;
　　　　　　LOVE AND CARE EVERYWHERE,
　　　　　　GOD ON PURPOSE SENDS YOU.

Shooting star and sunset shape the drama of creation,
Lightning flash and moonbeam share a common derivation.

Deserts stretch and torrents roar in contrast and confusion,
Tree tops shake and mountains soar and nothing is illusion.

All that flies and swims and crawls display an animation,
None can emulate or change for each has its own station.

Brother man and sister woman, born of dust and passion,
Praise the one who calls us friends and makes us in like fashion.

Kiss of life and touch of death suggest our imperfection;
Crib and womb and cross and tomb cry out for resurrection.

OR **'Christ be beside me'**

1. Christ be beside me,
Christ be before me,
Christ be behind me,
King of my heart.
Christ be within me,
Christ be below me,
Christ be above me,
never to part.

2. Christ on my right hand,
Christ on my left hand,
Christ all around me,
shield in the strife.
Christ in my sleeping,
Christ in my sitting,
Christ in my rising,
light of my life.

3. Christ be in all hearts
thinking about me,
Christ be in all tongues
telling of me.
Christ be the vision
in eyes that see me,
in ears that hear me,
Christ ever be.

Saturday **'Sing for God's glory'**

Sing for God's glory that colours the dawn of creation,
Racing across the sky trailing bright clouds of elation
Sun of delight succeeds the velvet of night
Warming the earth's exultation.

Sing for God's power that shatters the chains that would bind us,
Searing the darkness of fear and despair that could blind us,
Touching our shame with love that will not lay blame,
Reaching out gently to find us.

Sing for God's justice disturbing each easy illusion,
Tearing down tyrants and putting our pride to confusion,
Lifeblood of right, resisting evil and slight,
Offering freedom's transfusion.

Sing for God's saints who have travelled faith's journey before us,
Who, in our weariness, give us their hope to restore us,
In them we see the new creation to be,
Spirit of love made flesh for us.

OR   **'For the beauty of the Earth'**

1. For the beauty of the earth,
    For the beauty of the skies,
    For the love which from our birth
    Over and around us lies,
    CHRIST OUR GOD TO YOU WE RAISE
    THIS OUR SACRIFICE OF PRAISE.

2. For the joy of ear and eye,
    For the heart and mind's delight,
    For the mystic harmony
    Linking sense to sound and sight,

3. For the beauty of each hour
    Of the day and of the night,
    Hill and vale, and tree and flower,
    Sun and moon and stars of light,

Prayer of Confession

Leader: Holy God, Maker of all

ALL: HAVE MERCY ON US.

Leader: Jesus Christ, Servant of the poor

ALL: HAVE MERCY ON US.

Leader: Holy Spirit, Breath of life

ALL: HAVE MERCY ON US.

(Here the leader may offer a brief prayer of confession)

Leader: Let us in silence remember our own faults and failings.

Silence

Leader: I confess to God and in the company of all God's people that
my life and the life of the world are broken by my sin.

ALL: MAY GOD FORGIVE YOU, CHRIST RENEW YOU, AND THE
SPIRIT ENABLE YOU TO GROW IN LOVE.

Leader: Amen.

ALL: WE CONFESS TO GOD AND IN THE COMPANY OF ALL GOD'S
PEOPLE THAT OUR LIVES AND THE LIFE OF THE WORLD ARE
BROKEN BY OUR SIN.

Leader: May God forgive you, Christ renew you, and the Spirit enable
you to grow in love.

ALL: AMEN.

Prayer for God's Help

Leader: Turn again, O God, and give us life,

ALL: THAT YOUR PEOPLE MAY REJOICE IN YOU.

Leader: Make me a clean heart, O God,

ALL: AND RENEW A RIGHT SPIRIT WITHIN ME.

Leader: Give us again the joy of your help,

ALL: WITH YOUR SPIRIT OF FREEDOM SUSTAIN US.

(Here the leader may offer a brief prayer for God's help)

Leader: And now, as Jesus taught us, we say:

ALL: OUR FATHER IN HEAVEN,
HALLOWED BE YOUR NAME,
YOUR KINGDOM COME,
YOUR WILL BE DONE ON EARTH AS IN HEAVEN,
GIVE US TODAY OUR DAILY BREAD,
FORGIVE US OUR SINS
AS WE FORGIVE THOSE WHO SIN AGAINST US,
SAVE US FROM THE TIME OF TRIAL
AND DELIVER US FROM EVIL,
FOR THE KINGDOM, THE POWER AND THE GLORY ARE YOURS,
NOW AND FOR EVER. AMEN.

Psalm — *said responsively, the parts marked 'A' being read by those on the leader's side of the church, the parts marked 'B' being read by those on the opposite side, and so on.*

The Reading for the Day

Leader: This morning's passage comes from . . . . .
Listen now for the Word of God.

Reading *(After the reading, there is a period of silence, at the end of which the leader says)*

Leader: Thanks be to God.

ALL: AMEN.

Song of Praise

Prayers of Thanksgiving and Intercession

*(Here follow prayers of thanksgiving and of intercession:
for the church and the world,
for concerns of the Iona Community,
for members of the Iona Community and their families,
ending with:)*

Leader: May they not fail you,

ALL: NOR WE FAIL THEM.

15

(Then the leader says one of the following prayers:)

Monday O Christ, the Master Carpenter, who at the last, through wood and nails, purchased our whole salvation, wield well your tools in the workshop of your world, so that we who come rough-hewn to your bench may here be fashioned to a truer beauty of your hand. We ask it for your own name's sake.

ALL: AMEN.

Tuesday O God, you have set before us a great hope that your kingdom will come on earth, and have taught us to pray for its coming: make us ever ready to thank you for the signs of its dawning, and to pray and work for the perfect day when your will shall be done on earth as it is in heaven. Through Jesus Christ our Lord.

ALL: AMEN.

Wednesday O God, who brought us from the rest of last night to the new light of this day, bring us from the light of this day to the guiding light of eternity. Through Jesus Christ our Lord.

ALL: AMEN.

Thursday O Christ, you are within each of us. It is not just the interior of these walls: it is our own inner being you have renewed. We are your temple not made with hands. We are your body. If every wall should crumble, and every church decay, we are your habitation. Nearer are you than breathing, closer than hands and feet. Ours are the eyes with which you, in the mystery, look out in compassion on the world. Yet we bless you for this place, for your directing of us, your redeeming of us, and your indwelling. Take us outside, Lord, outside holiness, out to where soldiers curse and nations clash at the crossroads of the world. So shall this building continue to be justified. We ask it for your own name's sake.

ALL: AMEN.

Friday O God, our Father, who gave to your servant Columba the gifts of courage, faith and cheerfulness, and sent people forth from Iona to carry the word of your gospel to every creature, grant, we pray, a like spirit to your church, even at this present time. Further in all things the purpose of our community, that hidden things may be revealed to us, and new ways found to touch the hearts of all. May we preserve with each other sincere charity and peace, and, if it be your holy will, grant that this place of your abiding be continued still to be a sanctuary and a light. Through Jesus Christ our Lord.

ALL: AMEN.

Saturday   O God, lead us from death to life, from falsehood to truth. Lead us from despair to hope, from fear to trust. Lead us from hate to love, from war to peace. Let peace fill our hearts, our world, our universe. We ask it for your own name's sake.

ALL: AMEN.

Silence

Closing Responses *(All stand in preparation to leave)*

Leader: This is the day that God has made,
ALL: WE WILL REJOICE AND BE GLAD IN IT.

Leader: We will not offer to God
ALL: OFFERINGS THAT COST US NOTHING.

Leader: Go in peace and serve the Lord,
ALL: WE WILL SEEK PEACE AND PURSUE IT.

Leader: In the name of the Trinity of Love,
ALL: ONE GOD IN PERFECT COMMUNITY.
AMEN.

(We remain standing to leave, the work of our day flowing directly from our worship)

CONCERNING THE CELEBRATION OF COMMUNION

We celebrate Communion twice weekly in the Abbey Church, on Sunday morning and on Friday evening. Because we are an Ecumenical Community, ranging in any particular week from Quakers on the one hand through Church of Scotland and Anglicans to Roman Catholics on the other, we bring a wide range of traditions to this celebration. Some call it the Lord's Supper or the Holy Communion, while others refer to it as the Eucharist, the Mass or the Breaking of Bread. We believe that the invitation to this sacrament comes not from any church or individual, but from Jesus. We therefore invite in Christ's name all who hear his invitation and who wish to respond by receiving the bread and the wine. If for any reason people do not wish to receive the elements as they are distributed from hand to hand throughout the church we suggest that they simply pass the bread and the wine from their neighbour on one side to their neighbour on the other, and remain united with us in prayer.

On Sunday morning, when the Abbey Church is often filled with visitors and pilgrims from throughout the world, our service is a structured liturgy of celebrating the sacrament of Christ's Presence. On Friday evening, when we sit together around the long table set up in the Abbey Church, our service is a more intimate sharing of the Bread of Life, and a festive looking forward to the Kingdom of God when men and women will come from east and west, north and south, to sit at table together. Both services follow the four-fold action of Jesus at the last supper, when he took bread, blessed it, broke the bread and shared it and the wine.

Jesus took the bread and the wine. After the Word of God has been proclaimed the first action of our liturgy of communion is, in response, to offer the wine and the bread, baked in our Abbey kitchen. The elements are signs of the body of Jesus and of his self-giving, and are also signs of our offering. As members of Christ, the bread and wine which we offer as gifts of the earth and work of human hands also represent our bodies, our lives which again we bring to offer God. As

18

St. Augustine said to his people when they had placed the elements on the altar, 'there you are upon the table, there you are in the cup'.

Jesus blessed the bread and the wine. Just as Jesus was blessed with God's Spirit, so we, having offered ourselves, seek a blessing upon our lives and on the bread and wine; we seek a renewing of the life of Christ in us. It is a 're-membering' or 're-bodying' of Christ. It is over our lives as well as over the bread and wine that the words of blessing are spoken. As St. Chrysostom said, through the blessed food and drink we are renewed as 'flesh of Christ's flesh, and bone of Christ's bone'.

Jesus broke the bread and poured out the wine. In breaking the bread we remember the brokenness of Jesus' body on the cross and commit ourselves to travelling the path of sacrificial love. Jesus' words at the last supper, 'do this', challenge us not merely to break bread together but to open ourselves to the cost of discipleship. St. Paul wrote to the early Christians in Rome, 'present your bodies as a living sacrifice'. Just as on the road to Emmaus it was in the breaking of bread that the risen Christ was known to his disciples (Luke 24), so in the self-giving of our lives is Christ known to the world today.

Jesus shared the bread and the wine. During the distribution of the bread and wine we remember Jesus sharing his life with the disciples and with the poor and sick, and we are called to a sharing of our own lives and possessions with one another and the poor. The final blessing of the service returns us to where we began. As we begin by bringing all that we are into communion, so we end by taking our renewed selves back into the details of our common life. We follow the bread and wine out of church, and whether on a Sunday morning in the cloisters or on a Friday evening in the refectory we continue our celebration of communion out in the place of the ordinary. And in sharing ourselves with one another we share Christ.

SUNDAY MORNING COMMUNION

Opening Responses:

Leader: Thanks be to you O God, that we have risen this day,

ALL: TO THE RISING OF THIS LIFE ITSELF.

Leader: Be the purpose of God between us and each purpose,

ALL: THE HAND OF GOD BETWEEN US AND EACH HAND.

Leader: The pain of Christ between us and each pain,

ALL: THE LOVE OF CHRIST BETWEEN US AND EACH LOVE.

Leader: Beloved of the waifs, beloved of the naked,

ALL: DRAW US TO THE SHELTER-HOUSE OF THE SAVIOUR OF THE POOR.

Song   **'Jesus Calls Us'**

> Jesus calls us here to meet him
> As, through word and song and prayer,
> We affirm God's promised presence,
> Where his people live and care.
> Praise the God who keeps his promise,
> Praise the Son who calls us friends,
> Praise the Spirit who, among us,
> To our hopes and fears attends.
>
> Jesus calls us to confess him
> Word of Life and Lord of All,
> Sharer of our flesh and frailness,
> Saving all who fail or fall.
> Tell his holy human story,
> Tell his tales that all may hear,
> Tell the world that Christ in glory
> Came to earth to meet us here.

Jesus calls us to each other:
Found in him are no divides.
Race and class and sex and language,
Such are barriers he derides.
Join the hands of friend and stranger,
Join the hands of age and youth,
Join the faithful and the doubter
In their common search for truth.

Jesus calls us to his table,
Rooted firm in time and space,
Where the church in earth and heaven
Finds a common meeting place.
Share the bread and wine, his body,
Share the love of which we sing,
Share the feast for saints and sinners,
Hosted by our Lord and King.

Prayer — Confession and Invocation

Leader: God, holy:

ALL: GOD, STRONG AND HOLY,
GOD, HOLY AND DEATHLESS,
HAVE MERCY ON US.

Reading

Leader: Listen now, for God speaks to us in the Scriptures.

Reader: A reading from . . .

(after the reading, there is a period of silence, at the end of which the reader says . . .)

Reader: This is the word of the Lord.

ALL: THANKS BE TO GOD.

Song

(during the last verse of which children may leave for the cloisters or Chapter House)

Sermon

Offering

Affirmation of Faith *(The people standing)*

ALL: WE BELIEVE IN GOD ABOVE US,
MAKER AND SUSTAINER OF ALL LIFE,
OF SUN AND MOON,
OF WATER AND EARTH,
OF MALE AND FEMALE.
WE BELIEVE IN GOD BESIDE US,
JESUS CHRIST, THE WORD MADE FLESH,
BORN OF A WOMAN'S WOMB, SERVANT OF THE POOR.
HE WAS TORTURED AND NAILED TO A TREE.
A MAN OF SORROWS, HE DIED FORSAKEN.
HE DESCENDED INTO THE EARTH TO THE PLACE OF DEATH.
ON THE THIRD DAY HE ROSE FROM THE TOMB.
HE ASCENDED INTO HEAVEN TO BE EVERYWHERE PRESENT,
AND HIS KINGDOM WILL COME ON EARTH.
WE BELIEVE IN GOD WITHIN US,
THE HOLY SPIRIT OF PENTECOSTAL FIRE,
LIFE-GIVING BREATH OF THE CHURCH,
SPIRIT OF HEALING AND FORGIVENESS,
SOURCE OF RESURRECTION AND OF LIFE EVERLASTING.
AMEN.

OR

ALL: WE BELIEVE IN GOD, THE FATHER ALMIGHTY,
MAKER OF HEAVEN AND EARTH,
AND IN JESUS CHRIST, HIS ONLY SON, OUR LORD,
WHO WAS CONCEIVED BY THE HOLY GHOST,
BORN OF THE VIRGIN MARY,
SUFFERED UNDER PONTIUS PILATE,
WAS CRUCIFIED, DEAD, AND BURIED:
HE DESCENDED INTO HELL.
THE THIRD DAY HE ROSE AGAIN FROM THE DEAD,
HE ASCENDED INTO HEAVEN, AND SITS ON THE RIGHT
HAND OF GOD, THE FATHER ALMIGHTY:
FROM THENCE HE SHALL COME TO JUDGE THE QUICK AND
THE DEAD.
I BELIEVE IN THE HOLY GHOST;
THE HOLY CATHOLIC CHURCH;
THE COMMUNION OF SAINTS;
THE FORGIVENESS OF SINS;
THE RESURRECTION OF THE BODY;
AND THE LIFE EVERLASTING.   AMEN.

The Invitation

Communion Song   'The Hand of Heaven'

We, who live by sound and symbol,
We, who learn from sight and word,
Find these married in the person
Of the one we call our Lord.
Taking bread to be his body,
Taking wine to be his blood,
He let thought take flesh in action,
He let faith take root in food.

Not just once with special people,
Not just hidden deep in time,
But, wherever Christ is followed,
Earthly fare becomes sublime.
Though to sound this seems a mystery,
Though to sense it seems absurd,
Yet in faith, which seems like folly,
We meet Jesus Christ our Lord.

God, our Maker, send your Spirit
To pervade the bread we break.
Let it bring the life we long for
And the love which we forsake.
Bind us closer to each other,
Both forgiving and forgiven;
Give us grace in this and all things
To discern the hand of heaven.

The Story of the Last Supper

The Prayer of Thanks

Leader: The Lord be with you,

ALL: AND ALSO WITH YOU.

Leader: Lift up your hearts,

ALL: WE LIFT THEM UP TO GOD.

Leader: Let us give thanks to God,

ALL: IT IS RIGHT TO GIVE BOTH THANKS AND PRAISE.

Chant   *(each line to be repeated after the Cantor)*

Holy and One,	Glorious the heaven,	Blessed the One,
Holy in power,	Sacred the earth,	Come in your name,
Holy in energy,	Full of your clarity,	Highest Hosanna,
Glory to you.	Glory to you.	Glory to you.

OR

Holy, holy, holy, Lord of power and might,
Heaven, earth, heaven and earth are full of your glory,
All glory to your name.

Blessed, blessed is he who comes in the name of the Lord,
Blessed, blessed is he who comes in the name of the Lord.
Hosanna in the highest.

Prayers of Blessing and Intercession
(ending with the Lord's Prayer)

ALL: OUR FATHER IN HEAVEN,
HALLOWED BE YOUR NAME,
YOUR KINGDOM COME,
YOUR WILL BE DONE ON EARTH, AS IN HEAVEN.
GIVE US TODAY OUR DAILY BREAD.
FORGIVE US OUR SINS,
AS WE FORGIVE THOSE WHO SIN AGAINST US.
SAVE US FROM THE TIME OF TRIAL
AND DELIVER US FROM EVIL,
FOR THE KINGDOM, THE POWER AND THE GLORY ARE YOURS,
NOW AND FOR EVER.   AMEN.

The Sharing of the Bread and Wine

Chant   *(each line is repeated after the Cantor)*

O Lamb of God, you take away the sin of the world. Have mercy upon us.
O Lamb of God, you take away the sin of the world. Have mercy upon us.
O Lamb of God, you take away the sin of the world. Grant us your peace.

OR

Lamb of God, you take away the sin of the world. Have mercy upon us.
Lamb of God, you take away the sin of the world. Have mercy upon us.
Lamb of God, you take away the sin of the world. Grant us your peace.

A Sign of Peace

Leader: May the peace of Christ be with you,

ALL: AND ALSO WITH YOU.

Blessing

Leader: May the everlasting God shield you,
East and west and wherever you go.
And the blessing of God be upon us,

ALL: THE BLESSING OF THE GOD OF LIFE.

Leader: The blessing of Christ be upon us,

ALL: THE BLESSING OF THE CHRIST OF LOVE.

Leader: The blessing of the Spirit be upon us,

ALL: THE BLESSING OF THE SPIRIT OF GRACE.

Leader: The blessing of the Trinity be upon us.
Now and for ever more.

ALL: AMEN.

Closing Song   'Shout for Joy'

Shout for joy! The Lord has let us feast,
Heaven's own fare has fed the last and least;
Christ's own peace is shared again on earth;
God the Spirit fills us with new worth.

No more doubting, no more senseless dread:
God's good self has graced our wine and bread;
All the wonder heaven has kept in store
Now is ours to keep for evermore.

Celebrate with saints who dine on high,
Witnesses that love can never die.
'Hallelujah!' — thus their voices ring:
Nothing less in gratitude we bring.

Praise the Maker, praise the Maker's Son,
Praise the Spirit — three yet ever one;
Praise the God whose food and friends avow
Heaven starts here! The Kingdom beckons now!

(Following the service everyone is invited to come for tea in the cloisters. Also, as you leave the church, you will be handed a small piece of bread and invited to share it with a stranger. Through this ancient Columban tradition we continue our celebration together out in the place of the common life.)

A SERVICE OF WELCOME

Opening Responses

Leader: The God of heaven has made his home on earth,

ALL: CHRIST DWELLS AMONG US AND IS ONE WITH US.

Leader: Highest in all creation, he lives among the least,

ALL: HE JOURNIES WITH THE REJECTED AND WELCOMES THE
        WEARY.

Leader: Come now all who thirst

ALL: AND DRINK THE WATER OF LIFE.

Leader: Come now all who hunger

ALL: AND BE FILLED WITH GOOD THINGS.

Leader: Come now all who seek

ALL: AND BE WARMED BY THE FIRE OF LOVE.

Song   **'Come, Host of Heaven'**

> Come, Host of heaven's high dwelling place,
> Come, earth's disputed guest,
> Find in this house a welcome home,
> Stay here and take your rest.
>
> Surround these walls with faith and love,
> That through the nights and days,
> When human tongues from speaking cease,
> These stones may echo praise.
>
> Bless and inspire those gathered here
> With patience, hope and peace,
> And all the joys that know the depth
> In which all sorrows cease.

Here may the losers find their worth,
The strangers find a friend,
Here may the hopeless find their faith
And aimless find an end.

Build from the human fabric signs
Of how your kingdom thrives;
Of how the Holy Spirit changes life
Through changing lives.

So to the Lord whose care enfolds
The world held in his hands
Be glory, honour, love and praise
For which this house now stands.

Scripture Reading

Rune of Hospitality

Leader: Let us stand and say together the words of an old Celtic rune
of hospitality:

ALL: WE SAW A STRANGER YESTERDAY,
WE PUT FOOD IN THE EATING PLACE,
DRINK IN THE DRINKING PLACE,
MUSIC IN THE LISTENING PLACE
AND, WITH THE SACRED NAME OF THE TRIUNE GOD,
HE BLESSED US AND OUR HOUSE,
OUR CATTLE AND OUR DEAR ONES.

Leader: As the lark says in her song:
Often, often, often, goes Christ in the stranger's guise.

A Sign of Welcome   *(in which we greet the people next to us)*

Prayer and The Lord's Prayer

ALL: OUR FATHER IN HEAVEN,
HALLOWED BE YOUR NAME,
YOUR KINGDOM COME,
YOUR WILL BE DONE ON EARTH AS IN HEAVEN.
GIVE US TODAY OUR DAILY BREAD,
FORGIVE US OUR SINS
AS WE FORGIVE THOSE WHO SIN AGAINST US.
SAVE US FROM THE TIME OF TRIAL
AND DELIVER US FROM EVIL,
FOR THE KINGDOM, THE POWER AND THE GLORY ARE YOURS,
NOW AND FOR EVER. AMEN.

Song   **'The Love of God Comes Close'**

The love of God comes close
Where stands an open door
To let the stranger in,
To mingle rich and poor:
The love of God is here to stay,
Embracing those who walk his way.

The peace of God comes close
To those caught in the storm,
Forgoing lives of ease,
To ease the lives forlorn:
The peace of God is here to stay,
Embracing those who walk his way.

The joy of God comes close
Where faith encounters fears,
Where heights and depths of life
Are found through smiles and tears:
The joy of God is here to stay,
Embracing those who walk his way.

The grace of God comes close
To those whose grace is spent,
When hearts are tired or sore
And hope is bruised or bent:
The grace of God is here to stay,
Embracing those who walk his way.

Closing Prayer and Blessing

Chant   **'Night has Fallen'**

Leader: Night has fallen,

ALL: NIGHT HAS FALLEN,
          GRACIOUS SPIRIT, GUARD US SLEEPING.

Leader: Darkness now has come,

ALL: DARKNESS NOW HAS COME,
          GRACIOUS SPIRIT, GUARD US SLEEPING.

Leader: We are with you, God,

ALL: WE ARE WITH YOU, GOD,
          GRACIOUS SPIRIT, GUARD US SLEEPING.

Leader: See your children, God,

ALL: SEE YOUR CHILDREN, GOD,
GRACIOUS SPIRIT, GUARD US SLEEPING.

Leader: Keep us in your love,

ALL: KEEP US IN YOUR LOVE,
GRACIOUS SPIRIT, GUARD US SLEEPING.

Leader: Now we go to rest,

ALL: NOW WE GO TO REST,
GRACIOUS SPIRIT, GUARD US SLEEPING,
GRACIOUS SPIRIT, GUARD US SLEEPING.

SUNDAY EVENING QUIET TIME

Each Sunday evening at 9.00 p.m. a service of quiet and free prayer takes place for 20 minutes in the Abbey Church.

In order to help create and maintain an atmosphere of peace and quiet it is helpful to arrive a little early.

In the first part of this service, lasting for 15 minutes, we focus on an aspect of prayer to which many of us are not accustomed — that of listening to God. Much of our time spent in church emphasises the more active side of prayer and worship. We talk to God and often search for the most beautiful words in which to express our gratitude and concerns. However, in these quiet times we are trying to become more receptive to God — to create an atmosphere in which we are all more able to listen to what God is saying to us. We all know from our experience of listening to one another how difficult it often is to give each other our full attention. Distractions, both from the outside and from within, can prevent us from being fully present to the other. Listening to God is similar. Most of us lead very active lives and our minds and hearts reflect that busyness. It is very hard for us to let go of our concerns about the past, our anxieties for the future, important as they may be, and simply to be present to God. It calls for a kind of abandonment of our immediate cares in order to give space to a deeper listening to God. Whereas in other services we may focus on God as being above and beyond us, in the quiet time we turn our attention inwards to the God who dwells within each of us. There is no physical posture that is the right one in listening to God. Whether one sits or kneels or needs to shift position, the important thing is to remain alert to the Spirit of God within.

Spending time with God in quiet is not in any way an escape from the struggles of the world, for the God we encounter within is at the heart of the world's life and struggles as well. And in the listening to God we may encounter painful truths about ourselves which, if faced, will free us to be more fully of service to God in the world.

In the last 5 minutes we move from a period of silent communion with God into a time of free prayer and intercession. The leader of worship will pray for some members of the Iona Community who are being prayed for by the whole Community that day, and then will be silent. During this period anyone who feels moved to voice a prayer of intercession may do so. A suitable ending might be "GOD, IN YOUR MERCY" to which we can all respond, "HEAR OUR PRAYER".

The service ends with the saying of the *Nunc Dimittis* (Lk. 2):

Leader: Now, O God, may your servant go in peace
as you promised,
for my eyes have seen the salvation
which you have prepared for all to see,
a light to enlighten the nations
and the glory of your faithful people.

ALL: AMEN.

Those who wish to remain in prayer and quiet after the service ends are welcome to do so.

CONCERNING THE SERVICE OF PRAYER FOR JUSTICE AND PEACE

Every Monday evening in the Abbey Church we confessionally remember our part in the injustices of the world and pray for concerns which reflect the Justice and Peace commitment of the Iona Community. This commitment, which is an integral part of the Rule of the Community, stands as a 'point of departure' for us, and challenges us to action. In this service, we express our conviction that our prayers and our actions in this, as in all areas of our life, are two sides of the same coin.

"We believe:

1. that the Gospel commands us to seek peace founded on justice and that costly reconciliation is at the heart of the Gospel.

2. that work for justice, peace and an equitable society is a matter of extreme urgency.

3. that God has given us partnership as stewards of creation and that we have a responsibility to live in a right relationship with the whole of God's creation.

4. that, handled with integrity, creation can provide for the needs of all, but not for the greed which leads to injustice and inequality, and endangers life on earth.

5. that everyone should have the quality and dignity of a full life that requires adequate physical, social and political opportunity, without the oppression of poverty, injustice and fear.

6. that social and political action leading to justice for all people and encouraged by prayer and discussion, is a vital work of the Church at all levels.

7. that the use or threatened use of nuclear and other weapons of mass destruction is theologically and morally indefensible and that opposition to their existence is an imperative of the Christian faith.

"As members and Family Groups we will:

8. engage in forms of political witness and action, prayerfully and thoughtfully, to promote just and peaceful social, political and economic structures.

9. work for a British policy of renunciation of all weapons of mass destruction and for the encouragement of other nations, individually and collectively, to do the same.

10. work for the establishment of the United Nations Organisation as the principal organ of international reconciliation and security, in place of military alliances.

11. support and promote research and education into non-violent ways of achieving justice, peace and a sustainable global society.

12. work for reconciliation within and among nations by international sharing and exchange of experience and people, with particular concern for politically and economically oppressed nations."

A SERVICE OF PRAYER FOR JUSTICE AND PEACE

Welcome

Opening Responses

Leader: O God, who called all life into being,

ALL: THE EARTH, SEA AND SKY ARE YOURS.

Leader: Your presence is all around us,

ALL: EVERY ATOM IS FULL OF YOUR ENERGY.

Leader: Your Spirit enlivens all who walk the earth,

ALL: WITH HER WE YEARN FOR JUSTICE TO BE DONE,

Leader: For creation to be freed from bondage,

ALL: FOR THE HUNGRY TO BE FED,

Leader: For captives to be released,

ALL: FOR YOUR KINGDOM OF PEACE TO COME ON EARTH. AMEN.

Song

The Word
(readings, drama, symbolic actions with chants, etc. for Justice and Peace)

Affirmation of Faith

Leader: Let us celebrate and affirm our faith in the words of Mary's song: My heart praises you, O God,

ALL: MY SPIRIT REJOICES IN YOU MY SAVIOUR,

Leader: You have remembered me in my lowliness

ALL: AND NOW I WILL BE CALLED BLESSED.

Leader: You have done great things for me

ALL: AND SHOWN MERCY TO ALL THOSE WHO TRUST YOU.

Leader: You have stretched out your right arm

ALL: AND SCATTERED THE PROUD WITH ALL THEIR PLANS.

Leader: You have brought down the mighty from their thrones

ALL: AND LIFTED UP THE LOWLY.

Leader: You have filled the hungry with good things

ALL: AND SENT THE RICH AWAY WITH EMPTY HANDS.

Leader: You have kept your promise to our mothers and fathers

ALL: AND COME TO THE HELP OF YOUR PEOPLE, TO ABRAHAM
AND TO SARAH, AND TO ALL GENERATIONS FOR EVER. AMEN.

OR

ALL: I BELIEVE IN GOD, WHO IS LOVE AND WHO HAS GIVEN THE
EARTH TO ALL PEOPLE.

I BELIEVE IN JESUS CHRIST, WHO CAME TO HEAL US, AND TO
FREE US FROM ALL FORMS OF OPPRESSION.

I BELIEVE IN THE SPIRIT OF GOD, WHO WORKS IN AND
THROUGH ALL WHO ARE TURNED TOWARDS THE TRUTH.

I BELIEVE IN THE COMMUNITY OF FAITH, WHICH IS CALLED
TO BE AT THE SERVICE OF ALL PEOPLE.

I BELIEVE IN GOD'S POWER TO TRANSFORM AND
TRANSFIGURE, FULFILLING THE PROMISE OF A NEW HEAVEN
AND A NEW EARTH WHERE JUSTICE AND PEACE WILL
FLOURISH. AMEN.

Prayers of Confession/Intercession

Song

Closing Responses

Leader: A blessing on you who are poor,

ALL: YOURS IS THE KINGDOM OF GOD.

Leader: A blessing on you who mourn,

ALL: YOU SHALL BE COMFORTED.

Leader: A blessing on you who hunger for justice,

ALL: YOU SHALL BE SATISFIED.

Leader: A blessing on you who make peace,

ALL: YOU SHALL BE CALLED CHILDREN OF GOD.

Leader: A blessing on you who are persecuted in the cause of right,

ALL: YOURS IS THE KINGDOM OF HEAVEN.
AMEN.

CONCERNING PRAYERS FOR HEALING AND THE LAYING ON OF HANDS

During the service every Tuesday evening throughout the year, we include prayers for healing and the laying on of hands. We believe that Jesus calls those who follow him to a life of wholeness and that the ministry of healing is as much a part of Christian life as mission and service.

Prayers of Intercession

During the first part of the service prayers are said for people and places for whom prayer has been requested. Prayer was central to Jesus' ministry of love and healing, so when we pray for others we are joining with Him in the vital work of redeeming and transfiguring this world. Through intercession we are not seeking to change God but to change the world and praying that God's will should be done through us so that light and hope may be brought into places of darkness and despair.

If you wish to have an intercession included in the Tuesday evening service, please write the Christian name or the place name and a few details about the person or situation on a piece of paper and leave it in the box marked "intercessions" outside the Abbey office before 5.30 p.m. on Tuesdays. It is also possible to phone prayer requests to the Abbey office. Requests normally need to be renewed each week.

The Laying on of Hands

During the second part of the service our prayers focus on the congregation and there is an opportunity for everyone to share in and receive the ministry of prayer and the laying on of hands. The New Testament describes how Jesus and the early church not only prayed for the sick but also laid hands on them. We know in our own lives that touch can be comforting and healing. It can assure us that we are accepted and loved and can console us in our pain in a way that words alone cannot.

Each one of us is less than whole, yet because we belong to the Body of Christ we can also be instruments of healing, wounded healers for one another. And so everyone who wishes to receive prayer and to share in the ministry of the laying on of hands is invited to come forward. Those seeking prayer should take a place at one of the kneelers and those sharing in the laying on of hands should simply place a hand on the arm or shoulder of the person in front of or next to them. Others may prefer to remain seated and join in the words of the prayer for healing.

Process of Healing

In the story of Jesus healing the sick man by the pool of Bethesda (John 5) it was when the waters were troubled that the sick were healed. Similarly in our own lives it is often in our troubled times that we will be offered healing, even though we do not know the way in which God will do this. Jesus asked the man by the pool "Do you want to be healed?" to which the man indicated his willingness to be helped and changed, and he was healed.

Likewise we are invited to open our hearts to Jesus and let His love into the most painful places of our lives whether in body, mind or spirit. We then may begin to see our fragility and brokenness in a new light, not as aspects of ourselves of which we should be ashamed but in fact as ways through which Christ will come closer to us. There is nothing that God considers too trivial or too shameful to help us with. Our healing may not involve a cure, nor may our burden be taken away, but Christ will give us a new strength to bear it. And the things that cause us and other people to be hurt often require a political solution arising out of our prayer. Action and prayer belong together.

And, finally, we believe that the ministry of healing complements rather than replaces the work of medicine, which is also a gift of God. We also recognise that healing is not confined to this (or any other) service. Relationships, ideas, nature, work and creativity are other aspects of our lives through which God offers us healing.

The Iona Prayer Circle

Iona is the centre of a prayer fellowship of men and women from all over the world, committed to praying for people whose names are on our monthly intercessions list. Further information about joining the prayer circle, or about having a name added to the monthly list, can be obtained from the Prayer Circle Secretary, or from the Abbey Office.

A SERVICE OF PRAYER FOR HEALING

Welcome

Opening Responses

Leader: We come in this service to God,

ALL: IN OUR NEED, AND BRINGING WITH US THE NEEDS OF THE WORLD.

Leader: We come to God, who has come to us in Jesus,

ALL: AND WHO WALKS WITH US THE ROAD OF OUR WORLD'S SUFFERING.

Leader: We come with our faith and with our doubts;

ALL: WE COME WITH OUR HOPES AND WITH OUR FEARS.

Leader: We come as we are, because it is God who invites us to come,

ALL: AND GOD HAS PROMISED NEVER TO TURN US AWAY.

Song

Scripture Reading

Prayers of Intercession

The Invitation

Song   *(During the singing of this song, those who wish to receive prayer and the laying on of hands are asked to come and take a place at one of the kneelers set out, and those who wish to share in this ministry should also come out and stand behind those who kneel. If all the places are occupied, please wait with those standing, and after the first group have received the laying on of hands, they will move back to allow others to take their place.)*

Prayer for the Laying On of Hands

ALL: SPIRIT OF THE LIVING GOD, PRESENT WITH US NOW,
ENTER YOU, BODY, MIND AND SPIRIT,
AND HEAL YOU OF ALL THAT HARMS YOU,
IN JESUS' NAME. AMEN.

OR

(the following prayer in which one phrase is used at a time)

ALL: GOD TO ENFOLD YOU.

CHRIST TO TOUCH YOU.

THE SPIRIT TO SURROUND YOU.

Closing Prayer and Benediction

A CREATION LITURGY

Opening Responses

Leader: Let the light fall warm and red on the rock,
Let the birds sing their evening song
And let God's people say Amen.

ALL: AMEN.

Leader: Let the tools be stored away,
Let the work be over and done
And let God's people say Amen.

ALL: AMEN.

Leader: Let the flowers close and the stars appear,
Let hearts be glad and minds be calm
And let God's people say Amen.

ALL: AMEN.

Song

Psalm or Reading   *(concerning creation)*

Confession

Leader: O God, your fertile earth is slowly being stripped of its riches,

ALL: OPEN OUR EYES TO SEE.

Leader: O God, your living waters are slowly being choked with chemicals,

ALL: OPEN OUR EYES TO SEE.

Leader: O God, your clear air is slowly being filled with pollutants,

ALL: OPEN OUR EYES TO SEE.

Leader: O God, your creatures are slowly dying and your people are suffering,

ALL: OPEN OUR EYES TO SEE.

Leader: God our Maker, so move us by the wonder of creation,

ALL: THAT WE REPENT AND CARE MORE DEEPLY.

Leader: So move us to grieve the loss of life,

ALL: THAT WE LEARN TO CHERISH AND PROTECT YOUR WORLD.

Chant

(during which there will be an action in which we commit ourselves to caring for God's earth or celebrate the goodness of God's earth)

Prayer of Thanksgiving/Intercession

Song

Closing Responses

Leader: This we know, the earth does not belong to us,

ALL: WE BELONG TO THE EARTH.

Leader: This we know, all things are connected,

ALL: LIKE THE BLOOD THAT UNITES ONE FAMILY.

Leader: This we know, we did not weave the web of life,

ALL: WE ARE MERELY A STRAND IN IT.

Leader: This we know, whatever we do to the web,

ALL: WE DO TO OURSELVES.

Leader: Let us give thanks for the gift of creation,

ALL: LET US GIVE THANKS THAT ALL THINGS
HOLD TOGETHER IN CHRIST.

Blessing

Leader: Bless to us, O God,
The moon that is above us,
The earth that is beneath us,
The friends who are around us,
Your image deep within us,

ALL: AMEN.

CONCERNING THE ACT OF COMMITMENT SERVICE

'Will you come and follow me?' These are the words of Jesus that give shape to our Thursday evening liturgy. It is a simple service of personal commitment to Jesus in response to his love. For some it will be a commitment for the first time, while for others it will be a recommitment to the One whom they have been following as the Way, the Truth and the Life.

St. Augustine warned Christians of the 4th Century not to decapitate the risen Christ, that is, not to separate Jesus from the rest of his Body on earth, and therefore not to pretend that we can love Jesus while neglecting to love our brothers and sisters. On a Thursday evening the call for commitment to Jesus is at the same time a call for commitment to all that Jesus identifies himself with. We are not to separate what God has joined together, and so an act of commitment to Jesus is at the same time an act of commitment to the brothers and sisters throughout the world who journey with Jesus (1 John 4), just as it is a commitment to the suffering and the poor of the world with whom Jesus inseparably identified himself (Matt. 25), and to a care for the earth, sea and sky which God called into being through the Word (John 1).

By Thursday evening many in the Abbey Church will be thinking about the situations to which they will soon return. The act of commitment can be a way of confirming the new perspectives or healings or convictions that we have received on Iona, and thus help to prepare the path for integrating the Iona experience with our day to day situations.

During the service there is opportunity to make an outward sign of commitment by following the leader forward to the front of the church and, after affirming our faith, to kneel and receive the words and promises of Jesus.

While the call to commitment is spoken to each one of us, we respond in different ways and at different times. People should not feel under any obligation to move forward, or that not doing so is reflective of their level of commitment. Many choose to remain at prayer in their places to renew a commitment to Jesus. Everyone is encouraged to participate in the service in the way that is most helpful to them.

AN ACT OF COMMITMENT SERVICE

Welcome

Opening Responses

Leader: Jesus says, 'I am the Way for you'.

ALL: AND SO WE COME TO FOLLOW CHRIST.

Leader: Jesus says, 'I am the Truth for you'.

ALL: AND SO WE COME TO DWELL IN THE LIGHT.

Leader: Jesus says, 'I am the Life for you'.

ALL: AND SO WE COME, LEAVING BEHIND ALL ELSE TO WHICH
       WE CLING.

Song

Scripture

The Call to Commitment

Song   *(During the singing of the last verse, those who wish to make a
sign of commitment are invited to make their way to the table,
bringing this book with them)*

Affirmation of Faith

Leader: Let us affirm our faith.

ALL: WE BELIEVE IN JESUS CHRIST,
       SON OF THE ONE GOD,
       MAKER AND SUSTAINER OF EARTH, SEA AND SKY.

       BORN OF MARY'S WOMB,
       FAITHFUL TO THE GOD OF ABRAHAM AND SARAH,
       JESUS HEALED THE SICK,
       SERVED THE POOR,
       AND PROCLAIMED HEAVEN ON EARTH.

CONDEMNED BY THE RELIGIOUS,
CRUCIFIED BY THE STATE,
HE DIED
BUT TRANSFORMED EVEN DEATH
AND ROSE TO LIFE EVERLASTING.

HE BLESSED THE DISCIPLES WITH HIS HOLY SPIRIT AND
SENT THEM FORTH, EAST AND WEST, NORTH AND SOUTH.

WE COMMIT OURSELVES
TO JESUS,
TO ONE ANOTHER AS BROTHERS AND SISTERS
AND TO HIS MISSION IN THE WORLD
IN THE GRACE OF THE HOLY SPIRIT.
AMEN.

Prayer

Words of Jesus *(during which the promises and commands of Jesus will be said over each person making a sign of commitment. The act of commitment will close with the following response:)*

Leader: May God bless you and keep you,
May God's face shine on you and give you grace,
May God's eyes light upon you and bring you peace.

ALL: AMEN.

Song *(during which people may return to their seats)*

Closing Responses

Leader: Look at your hands, see the touch and the tenderness,

ALL: GOD'S OWN FOR THE WORLD.

Leader: Look at your feet, see the path and the direction,

ALL: GOD'S OWN FOR THE WORLD.

Leader: Look at your heart, see the fire and the love,

ALL: GOD'S OWN FOR THE WORLD.

Leader: Look at the cross, see God's Son and our Saviour,

ALL: GOD'S OWN FOR THE WORLD.

Leader: This is God's world,

ALL: AND WE WILL SERVE GOD IN IT.

Leader: May God bless you, may God keep you always,
And lead your lives with love.

ALL: AMEN.

(As you leave the church there is opportunity to make an offering towards the work of the Iona Community)

AN EVENING SERVICE OF COMMUNION

Welcome

Opening Responses

1st Voice: I will light a light in the name of the Maker,
Who lit the world and breathed the breath of life for me.

2nd Voice: I will light a light in the name of the Son,
Who saved the world and stretched out his hand to me.

3rd Voice: I will light a light in the name of the Spirit,
Who encompasses the world and blesses my soul with yearning.

ALL: WE WILL LIGHT THREE LIGHTS FOR THE TRINITY OF LOVE:
GOD ABOVE US, GOD BESIDE US, GOD BENEATH US:
THE BEGINNING, THE END, THE EVERLASTING ONE.

Prayer of Invocation

Song

The Word *(Scripture readings, reflections, drama, movement, etc.)*

Chant   *(or song)*

The Invitation

Communion Song

Story of The Last Supper

Prayer of Thanksgiving *(Ending with the singing of the 'Holy, Holy')*

The Blessing of the Bread and Wine

Prayers of Intercession
(during which there is opportunity to offer free prayer in one's
own language, followed by the people's sung response)

The Breaking and Sharing of the Bread and Wine

(during which we serve one another around the table with the Bread and Wine)

A Sign of Peace

(during which there is opportunity to greet one another with a Sign of Peace)

Closing Responses

Leader: On our hearts and on our houses,

ALL: THE BLESSING OF GOD.

Leader: In our coming and our going,

ALL: THE PEACE OF GOD.

Leader: In our life and our believing,

ALL: THE LOVE OF GOD.

Leader: At our end and new beginning,

ALL: THE ARMS OF GOD TO WELCOME US AND BRING US HOME. AMEN.

Chant *(or song)*

AN ALTERNATIVE COMMUNION LITURGY

The Drama of Creation

Leader: In the beginning, God made the world:

Women: Made it and mothered it,

Men: Shaped it and fathered it;

Women: Filled it with seed and with signs of fertility,

Men: Filled it with life and with song and variety.

Leader: All that is green, blue, deep and growing,

ALL: GOD'S IS THE HAND THAT CREATED YOU.

Leader: All that is tender, firm, fragrant and curious,

ALL: GOD'S IS THE HAND THAT CREATED YOU.

Leader: All that crawls, flies, swims, walks or is motionless,

ALL: GOD'S IS THE HAND THAT CREATED YOU.

Leader: All that speaks, sings, cries, laughs or keeps silence,

ALL: GOD'S IS THE HAND THAT CREATED YOU.

Leader: All that suffers, lacks, limps or longs for an end,

ALL: GOD'S IS THE HAND THAT CREATED YOU.

Leader: The world belongs to God,

ALL: THE EARTH AND ALL ITS PEOPLE.

Prayer of Invocation

Song

The Drama of Incarnation

Leader: When the time was right, God sent the Son.

Women: Sent him and suckled him,

Men: Reared him and risked him;

Women: Filled him with laughter and tears and compassion,

Men: Filled him with anger and love and devotion.

Leader: Unwelcomed child, refugee and runaway,

ALL: CHRIST IS GOD'S OWN SON.

Leader: Skilled carpenter and homeless wayfarer,

ALL: CHRIST IS GOD'S OWN SON.

Leader: Feeder and teacher, healer and antagonist,

ALL: CHRIST IS GOD'S OWN SON.

Leader: Lover of the unlovable, toucher of the untouchable, forgiver of the unforgivable,

ALL: CHRIST IS GOD'S OWN SON.

Leader: Loved by the least, feared by the leaders; befriended by the weak, despised by the strong; deserted by his listeners, denied by his friends; bone of our bone, flesh of our flesh, writing heaven's pardon over earth's mistakes,

ALL: CHRIST IS GOD'S OWN SON.

Leader: The Word became flesh,

ALL: HE LIVED AMONG US, HE WAS ONE OF US.

The Word
(Scripture readings, reflections, drama, movement etc.)

The Drama of Salvation

Leader: When the world could wait no longer,

Women: The carpenters took up their tools,

Men: They made a cross for God's own Son,

Women: Fashioned from wood and skill of human hands,

Men: Fashioned from hate and will of human minds.

Leader: He was a man of sorrows and acquainted with grief,

ALL: FOR US HE GRIEVED.

Leader: He was summoned to the judgement hall,
an enemy of the state, a danger to religion,

ALL: BY US HE WAS JUDGED.

Leader: He was lashed with tongues and scourged with thongs,

ALL: BY HIS STRIPES WE ARE HEALED.

Leader: He was nailed to the cross by human hands,

ALL: BONE OF OUR BONE, FLESH OF OUR FLESH.

Leader: He died, declaring God's forgiveness. He rose on the third day,
transforming death. He ascended into heaven, that he might
be everywhere on earth. He sent the Holy Spirit as the seal of
his intention. He sets before us bread and wine, and invites us
to his table. This is the place where we are made well again.

ALL: AND ALL WILL BE MADE WELL.

Leader: For God sent the Son into the world not to condemn the world,

ALL: BUT THAT THE WORLD THROUGH HIM MIGHT BE SAVED.

The Invitation

Song

The Story of The Last Supper

Prayer of Thanksgiving *(ending with 'Holy Holy')*

The Blessing of the Bread and Wine

The Prayers of Intercession
(during which there is opportunity to offer prayer in ones own language, followed by the people's sung response)

The Breaking and Sharing of the Bread and Wine
(during which we serve one another around the table with the Bread and Wine)

The Sign of Peace

The Drama of Celebration

Leader: In the end as in the beginning, God is God:

Women: Loved by us, wanted by us,

Men: Praised by us, served by us;

Women: Filling the folk with the gifts of the Spirit,

Men: Making them whole for the good of the earth.

Leader: For bread and wine, this place and this time,

ALL: THANKS BE TO GOD.

Leader: For the peace we are promised which the world won't destroy,

ALL: THANKS BE TO GOD.

Leader: For the hope of heaven on earth and the final song of joy,

ALL: THANKS BE TO GOD.

Blessing

Chant   *(or song)*

A SIMPLE EVENING LITURGY

Opening Responses

Leader: Peace on each one who comes in need,

ALL: PEACE ON EACH ONE WHO COMES IN JOY.

Leader: Peace on each one who offers prayers,

ALL: PEACE ON EACH ONE WHO OFFERS SONG.

Leader: Peace of the Maker, Peace of the Son,

ALL: PEACE OF THE SPIRIT, THE TRIUNE ONE.

Song

Prayer

Leader: O God, for your love for us, warm and brooding,
which has brought us to birth and opened our eyes
to the wonder and beauty of creation,

ALL: WE GIVE YOU THANKS.

Leader: For your love for us, wild and freeing,
which has awakened us to the energy of creation:
to the sap that flows,
the blood that pulses,
the heart that sings.

ALL: WE GIVE YOU THANKS.

Leader: For your love for us, compassionate and patient,
which has carried us through our pain,
wept beside us in our sin,
and waited with us in our confusion.

ALL: WE GIVE YOU THANKS.

Leader: For your love for us, strong and challenging,
which has called us to risk for you,
asked for the best in us,
and shown us how to serve.

ALL: WE GIVE YOU THANKS.

Leader: O God we come to celebrate
that your Holy Spirit is present deep within us,
and at the heart of all life.
Forgive us when we forget your gift of love
made known to us in Jesus,
and draw us into your presence.

The Word of God

Song

Sharing of the Day   *(The leader invites the company to share a brief word or picture from today which is special in some way)*

Prayer

(Here is opportunity for prayers of concern, spoken or unspoken — each prayer being followed by a chant)

We bring to God someone whom we have met or remembered today and for whom we want to pray
(Chant)

We bring to God someone who is hurting tonight and needs our prayer
(Chant)

We bring to God a troubled situation in our world tonight
(Chant)

We bring to God silently, someone whom we find hard to forgive or trust
(Chant)

We bring ourselves to God
that we might grow in generosity of spirit,
clarity of mind,
and warmth of affection.
(Chant)

Song

Closing Responses

Leader: O Trinity of Love,
You have been with us at the world's beginning,

ALL: BE WITH US TILL THE WORLD'S END.

Leader: You have been with us at our life's shaping,

ALL: BE WITH US AT OUR LIFE'S END.

Leader: You have been with us at the sun's rising,

ALL: BE WITH US TILL THE DAY'S END.
AMEN.

Blessing

A CELTIC EVENING LITURGY

Opening Responses

Leader: Come to us this night, O God,

ALL: COME TO US WITH LIGHT
(here a candle may be lit and placed centrally)

Leader: Speak to us this night, O God,

ALL: SPEAK TO US YOUR TRUTH.
(here a bible may be placed centrally)

Leader: Dwell with us this night, O God,

ALL: DWELL WITH US IN LOVE.
(here a cross may be placed centrally)

Song

Prayer of Thanksgiving

Leader: Thanks be to you O Christ,

ALL: FOR THE MANY GIFTS YOU HAVE BESTOWED ON US,
EACH DAY AND NIGHT, EACH SEA AND LAND,
EACH WEATHER FAIR, EACH CALM, EACH WILD.

Leader: Each night may we remember your mercy
given so gently and generously.

ALL: EACH THING WE HAVE RECEIVED, FROM YOU IT CAME;
EACH THING FOR WHICH WE HOPE, FROM YOUR LOVE IT
WILL COME; EACH THING WE ENJOY, IT IS OF YOUR BOUNTY;
EACH THING WE ASK, COMES OF YOUR DISPOSING.

Leader: O God, from whom each thing that is, freely flows,

ALL: GRANT THAT NO TIE OVER STRICT, NO TIE OVER DEAR,
MAY BE BETWEEN OURSELVES AND THIS WORLD.
AMEN.

The Word of God

Leader: O God, as these words are read,

ALL: IN OUR HEARTS MAY WE FEEL YOUR PRESENCE.

Reader: (a portion of scripture read clearly)

Song

Affirmation of Faith

ALL: WE BELIEVE, O GOD OF ALL GODS,
THAT YOU ARE THE ETERNAL GOD OF LIFE,
WE BELIEVE, O GOD OF ALL GODS,
THAT YOU ARE THE ETERNAL GOD OF LOVE.

Men: We believe, O God and Maker of all creation,
That you are the creator of the high heavens,
That you are the creator of the deep seas,
That you are the creator of the stable earth.

Women: We believe, O God of all the peoples,
That you created our souls and set their warp,
That you created our bodies and gave them breath,
That you made us in your own image.

ALL: WE ARE GIVING YOU WORSHIP WITH OUR WHOLE LIVES,
WE ARE GIVING YOU ASSENT WITH OUR WHOLE POWER,
WE ARE GIVING YOU OUR EXISTENCE WITH OUR WHOLE MIND,
WE ARE GIVING YOU KNEELING WITH OUR WHOLE DESIRE.

Prayers of Concern

Leader: O Christ, kindle in our hearts within
A flame of love to our neighbour,
To our foes, to our friends, to our kindred all.

ALL: O CHRIST OF THE POOR AND THE YEARNING,
FROM THE HUMBLEST THING THAT LIVES
TO THE NAME THAT IS HIGHEST OF ALL,
KINDLE IN OUR HEARTS WITHIN
A FLAME OF LOVE.
*(Here a ring of votive candles may be lit around the symbols,
followed by a period of silence)*

OR

*(Each person may have a candle which will be lit from neighbour
to neighbour, followed by a period of intercessions, freely spoken
or unspoken)*

(At the end of this time the following prayer will be said:)

Leader: We are placing our souls and our bodies
Under your guarding this night, O Christ.

ALL: O SON OF THE TEARS, OF THE WOUNDS, OF THE PIERCINGS,
MAY YOUR CROSS THIS NIGHT BE SHIELDING ALL.

Song

Blessing

Leader: Be the great God between your shoulders
To protect you in your going and your coming;
Be the Son of Mary near your heart;
And be the perfect Spirit upon you pouring.

ALL: AMEN.

AFTERNOON PRAYERS FOR JUSTICE AND PEACE

Welcome

Opening Responses

Leader: We are called from the ends of the earth,

ALL: WE ARE CALLED FROM THE CENTRE OF OUR LIVES.

Leader: Men and women, young and old,

ALL: RICH AND POOR, STRONG AND WEAK.

Leader: We are called into God's love,

ALL: TO YEARN FOR JUSTICE AND TO PRAY FOR PEACE.
AMEN.

Reading

Song

Prayers and Blessings

Monday *(prayers concerning the use of violence and intercessions for peace, along with the following)*

O God, lead us from death to life,
from falsehood to truth.
Lead us from despair to hope,
from fear to trust.
Lead us from hate to love,
from war to peace.
Let peace fill our hearts,
our world, our universe. Amen.
(The Universal Prayer for Peace)

Leader: Peace to the nations, east and west,
Peace to our neighbours, black and white,
Peace to all women, peace to all men,
The peace of Christ above all peace.

ALL: AMEN.

Tuesday *(prayers concerning the inequities of wealth and resources in the world and intercessions for the hungry, along with the following)*

Make us worthy, O Lord, to serve the men and women throughout the world who live and die in poverty and hunger. Give them, through our hands, this day their daily bread, and by our understanding and love, give peace and joy.   Amen.
(Mother Teresa)

Leader: And now may the God of peace give you peace at all times and in all ways.

ALL: AMEN.

Wednesday *(prayers concerning environmental abuse and intercessions for creation, along with the following)*

O Christ, there is no plant in the ground
But it is full of your virtue.
There is no form in the strand
But it is full of your blessing.
There is no life in the sea,
There is no creature in the ocean,
There is nothing in the heavens
But proclaims your goodness.
There is no bird on the wing,
There is no star in the sky,
There is nothing beneath the sun
But proclaims your goodness. Amen.
(A Celtic Prayer)

Leader: Deep peace of the running wave to you,
Deep peace of the flowing air to you,
Deep peace of the quiet earth to you,
Deep peace of the shining stars to you,
Deep peace of the Son of Peace to you.

ALL: AMEN.

Thursday *(prayers concening repressive political regimes and intercessions for the oppressed and prisoners of conscience, along with the following)*

Lord Jesus, you experienced torture and death as a prisoner of conscience. You were beaten and flogged, and sentenced to an agonising death though you had done no wrong.
Be now with prisoners of conscience throughout the world. Be with them in their fear and loneliness in the agony of physical and mental torture, and in the face of execution and death. Stretch out your hands in power to break their chains. Be merciful to the oppressor and the torturer, and place a new heart within them. Forgive all injustice in our lives, and transform us to be instruments of your peace, for by your wounds we are healed.   Amen.
(Amnesty International)

Leader: And now may the peace of God, which passes all understanding, guard your hearts and your thoughts,in Christ Jesus.

ALL: AMEN.

Friday *(prayers concerning economic exploitation and the lack of equal opportunity and intercessions for victims of injustice and the unemployed, along with the following)*

Lord, make us instruments of your peace.
Where there is hatred, let us sow love,
Where there is injury, pardon,
Where there is doubt, faith,
Where there is despair, hope,
Where there is sadness, joy.
O Divine Master,
Grant that we may not so much
Seek to be consoled as to console,
To be understood as to understand,
To be loved as to love.
For it is in giving that we receive,
It is in pardoning that we are pardoned,
It is in dying that we are born again
To everlasting life. Amen.
(St. Francis)

Leader: And now may the God of hope bring you such joy and peace in believing that you overflow with hope in the power of the Holy Spirit.

ALL: AMEN.

Saturday *(prayers concerning political and economic instability and intercessions for refugees and the homeless, along with the following)*

O Brother Jesus, who as a child was carried into exile,
Remember all those who are deprived of their home or country,
Who groan under the burden of anguish and sorrow,
Enduring the burning heat of the sun,
The freezing cold of the sea, or the humid heat of the forest,
Searching for a place of refuge.
Cause these storms to cease, O Christ.
Move the hearts of those in power
That they may respect the men and women
Whom you have created in your own image;
That the grief of refugees may be turned into joy,
As when you led Moses and your people out of captivity. Amen.
(African Prayer for Refugees)

Leader: May God bless you and keep you,
May God's face shine on you and give you grace,
May God's eyes light upon you and bring you peace.

ALL: AMEN.

THE IONA PILGRIMAGE

Over the centuries millions of pilgrims have come to this cradle of Christianity in Scotland, seeking healing, inspiration and new beginnings. And all have been received here, whether rich or poor, old or young.

On Wednesdays everyone on Iona is welcome to join the pilgrimage around the island, visiting places of historical and religious significance and reflecting on the journey of our lives and the life of the world. At each station there is a brief reflection and prayer, and sometimes silence or songs.

The Pilgrimage begins at 10.15 a.m. at the foot of St. Martin's Cross by the west door of the Abbey Church, and ends in St. Oran's Chapel at approximately 4.00 p.m. A packed lunch is provided for the guests of the Iona Community, and a cup of tea is provided for all at the Machair. Strong footwear and a warm waterproof coat are recommended. The pilgrimage path is often rough and wet underfoot. People may if they wish only do part of the day's journey, in which case it is simplest either to join us for the first half and depart after lunch, or arrive for lunch at the Machair (around 1.00 p.m.) for the second half.

St. Martin's Cross has marked this place of pilgrimage for over a thousand years. It is named after St. Martin, a fourth century Roman soldier, who in sharing his clothing with a poor man received a vision of Christ. After his baptism he became known for his conscientious objection to serving in the Roman army, and later, as the Bishop of Tours, played an important role in the mission to the Celts. The high standing crosses of the Celtic Church suggest that worship often occurred out in the midst of the wide worship of earth, sea and sky. And the Celtic everlasting pattern of the weaving vine on the cross points to the intertwining of heaven and earth. As George MacLeod, founder of the Iona Community, says of Iona, 'It is a very thin place. There is only a thin separation between spirit and matter.' On our Iona pilgrimage we look for the spiritual at the heart of the physical world.

Bless to us, O God,
The earth beneath our feet.
Bless to us, O God,
The path whereon we go.
Bless to us, O God,
The people whom we meet.
Amen.

The Augustinian Nunnery was built around the same time as the 13th century Benedictine Abbey. One can imagine the nuns worshipping in the nave of the little chapel, sharing meals in the refectory, and meeting in the Chapter House, but, although we can imagine these things, there is in fact very little historical record of the life of the women living and worshipping together on this island. History has provided us with an almost total focus on the Abbey. The lack of historical attention to the Nunnery reflects the neglect of women in a society and church of male domination for centuries. Hand in hand with the subordination of women has often gone a neglect of the earth, and an abuse of the human body.

One of the offerings of the ancient Celtic Church to today is its greater balance between the feminine and masculine, as well as its celebration of the interweaving of matter and spirit, and its affirmation of the goodness of creation and the human body. St. Brigid, for instance, in her leadership of double monasteries of men and women in the Celtic Church, stands for us as a model of equality between men and women.

Bless to us, O God,
Our souls that come from on high.
Bless to us, O God,
Our bodies that are of earth.
Bless to us, O God,
Each thing our eyes see.
Bless to us, O God,
Each sound our ears hear.
Bless to us, O God,
Each odour that goes to our nostrils.
Bless to us, O God,
Each taste that goes to our lips,
Each note that goes to our song,
Each ray that guides our way.
Amen.

The Marble Quarry, situated near the south-east corner of the island, is where the Benedictines may have carved their high altar. And it was here that the white Iona marble with green streaks of serpentine was quarried for the present day communion table and baptismal font of the Abbey Church. Situated above some of the oldest stone in the world, the marble quarry reminds us of earth's evolution over hundreds of millions of years, of our place in creation's history and our responsibility to care for the earth. The rusty metal scaffolding and heaps of abandoned stone in the quarry speak of a type of disrespect for the environment which we see on a much larger scale elsewhere in the world. In the Marble Quarry we reflect confessionally on the situations in our world where natural resources have been exploited, and where human lives have been broken and left in a heap all in the pursuit of wealth and power, and here we give thanks for the goodness of creation.

> O Christ, there is no plant in the ground
> But it is full of your virtue.
> There is no form in the strand
> But it is full of your blessing.
> There is no life in the sea,
> There is no creature in the ocean,
> There is nothing in the heavens
> But proclaims your goodness.
> There is no bird on the wing,
> There is no star in the sky,
> There is nothing beneath the sun
> But proclaims your goodness.
> Amen.

St. Columba's Bay is the pebbled beach at the southern tip of the island where Columba is said to have arrived from Ireland on Pentecost Day in the year 563. Having clambered up the beach with their leather-bound boat, known as a coracle, legend has it that Columba and his twelve monks climbed the hill to the west of the bay to confirm that Ireland, their beloved home country, could not be seen. 'The Hill of Turning the Back to Ireland' became a landmark for them as they moved forward in mission. They established their monastic centre on the east side of the island around the present day site of the Abbey, and from there conducted a mission to the Picts in the north, to the Anglo-Saxons in Northumbria, and throughout Europe, reaching as far east as western Russia. St. Columba's Bay is a place of leaving behind the past and of new beginnings in pilgrimage and mission.

> And now, may kindly Columba guide you
> To be an isle in the sea,
> To be a hill on the shore,
> To be a star in the night,
> To be a staff for the weak.
> Amen.

The Machair, which simply means 'raised beach', is the common land on the west side of the island overlooking the 'Bay at the Back of the Ocean'. For centuries it was used as the cornfield for the Celtic monastery and later by the Benedictines. Now it is a field used in turn by the farmers for common grazing. So the Machair is like a parable of sharing, of co-operation as opposed to competition. Here we share our lunch together and give thanks, remembering that we are called to share the gifts of God with one another and with the poor of the world.

Each thing we have received,
From you it came, O God.
Each thing for which we hope,
From your love it will be given.
Kindle in our hearts within
A flame of love to our neighbours,
To our foes, to our friends, to our loved ones all,
From the lowliest thing that lives,
To the name that is highest of all.
Amen.

The Hermit's Cell, now only a secluded ring of stones, is situated towards the north of the island. These stones may be the remains of a Celtic beehive hut, used over the centuries as a place of solitude. There are accounts of Columba spending time alone in prayer on the island, and it may be that this was his place of hermitage. Times of solitude and silence undergird the busyness and demands of living interwoven in community. As well as hearing the word of God through the scriptures, through creation and through one another, we can experience the word of God deep within us at the very heart of all being.

Deep peace of the running wave to you,
Deep peace of the flowing air to you,
Deep peace of the quiet earth to you,
Deep peace of the shining stars to you,
Deep peace of the Son of Peace to you.
Amen.

Dun I, which simply means the hill of Iona, is the highest point on the island, 102 metres above sea level. On a clear day one can see The Cuillins of Skye to the north, Ben More to the east, the Paps of Jura to the south, and the lighthouse of Skerryvore to the west, several miles off Tiree. Closer to the north lie the Treshnish Isles and the Island of Staffa. At the north-eastern tip of the island is the White Strand of the Monks, where late in the 9th century there was a martyrdom of the Abbot and fifteen monks. And earlier in that century at Martyrs Bay sixty-eight monks had been slaughtered at the hands of Norse invaders. Iona, the holy island of peace, has known its own bloodshed and struggle.

In the biblical tradition, mountains or hills have been understood as places of new vision and transfiguration. Also in the bible the sea is portrayed as a place of risk, which can suddenly and unpredictably blow into storm. If Iona is like a hilltop experience of new perspective then often the places that we return to are more like the dangerous seas. On Dun I we begin to refocus on those places of struggle in our world that we belong to and are aware of, and we offer a prayer for peace.

> Peace between nations,
> Peace between neighbours,
> Peace between lovers,
> In love of the God of life.
> Peace between person and person,
> Peace between wife and husband,
> Peace between parent and child,
> The peace of Christ above all peace.
> Bless O Christ our faces,
> Let our faces bless everything,
> Bless O Christ our eyes,
> Let our eyes bless all they see.
> Amen.

St. Oran's Chapel, just inside the main gate of the Abbey grounds, is the oldest building on Iona. It was restored in the 11th century at the request of St. Margaret, Queen of Scots. Oran is remembered as the first Columban monk to die and be buried on Iona.

The area became known as the Reilig Oran (or the graveyard of Oran). Many Scottish Kings and Lords of the Isles, as well as Irish and Norse Kings, are said to be buried here. A graveyard may seem an odd place to end the Iona pilgrimage, but in the Christian Church we celebrate that it was in a graveyard that the resurrection faith began, and it is often in places of death and apparent hopelessness that new beginnings are given. Our prayer is that through the self-giving and deaths of Oran and Columba and the many other women and men who have gone before us we may be granted the strength and vision to continue on the journey of Jesus.

> May the eye of God be dwelling with you,
> The foot of Christ in guidance with you,
> The shower of the Spirit pouring on you,
> Richly and generously.
> Amen.

APPENDIX FOR THE SUNDAY MORNING COMMUNION

Prayer of Confession

Leader: Holy God, maker of the skies above,
Lowly Christ, born amidst the growing earth,
Spirit of life, wind over the flowing waters,
In earth, sea and sky,
You are there.

O hidden mystery,
Sun behind all suns,
Soul behind all souls,
In everything we touch,
In everyone we meet,
Your presence is round us,
And we give you thanks.

But when we have not touched, but trampled you in creation,
When we have not met but missed you in one another,
When we have not received but rejected you in the poor,
Forgive us,
And hear now our plea for mercy.

Prayer of Invocation

Leader: Come, Father of the poor,
Come, Light of our hearts,
Come, generous Spirit,
By the glory of your creation around us,
By the comfort of your forgiveness within us,
By the wind of your Spirit eddying through the
centuries within these walls,
Renew us,
So that we come glad to this celebration.
Amen.

The Invitation

Leader: The table of bread and wine is now to be made ready.
It is the table of company with Jesus
And with all those who love him.
It is the table of sharing with the poor of the world,
With whom Jesus identified himself.
It is the table of communion with the earth
In which Christ became incarnate.

So, come to this table,
You who have much faith
And you who would like to have more;
You who have been to this sacrament often,
And you who have not been for a long time;
You who have tried to follow Jesus,
And you who have failed.
Come.
It is Christ who invites us to meet him here.

The Story of The Last Supper

Leader: Blessed is our brother Jesus,
Who walks with us the road of our world's suffering,
And who is known to us in the breaking of bread.
On the night of his arrest Jesus took bread
And having blessed it
He broke the bread
And gave it to his disciples, saying,
'This is my body, given for you'.
In the same way he took wine
And having given thanks for it
He poured it out
And gave the cup to his disciples, saying,
'This cup is the new relationship with God,
Sealed with my blood.
Take this and share it.
I shall drink wine with you next
In the coming Kingdom of God.'

Loving God,
It is through your goodness that we have
This bread and wine to offer,
Which earth has given and human hands have made.
In the sharing of this bread,
May we know your resurrection presence,
And may we know that, in touching all bread, all matter,
It is you that we touch.

What we do here is celebrate the life that Jesus has shared
Among his community through the centuries
And shares among us now.
Made one with Christ
And thus one with each other,
Let us offer these gifts and with them ourselves,
A single, holy, living sacrifice.

The Lord be with you . . . .

The Prayer of Thanksgiving

Leader: We offer you praise, dear God,
And hearts lifted high,
For in the communion of your love
Christ comes close to us
And we come close to Christ.

Therefore with the whole realm of nature around us,
With earth, sea and sky,
We sing to you.

With the angels of light who envelop us,
With Michael and the host of heaven,
With all the saints before and beside us,
With Columba and Brigid, Patrick and Margaret,
With brothers and sisters, east and west,
We sing to you.

And with our loved ones,
Separate from us now,
Who yet in this mystery are close to us,
We join in the song of your unending greatness.

Prayer of Blessing

Leader: Hear us now, O Christ,
And breathe your Spirit upon us
And upon this bread and wine.
May they become for us your body,
Vibrant with your life,
Healing, renewing and making us whole.
And as the bread and wine which we now eat and drink
Are changed into us,
May we be changed again into you,
Bone of your bone,
Flesh of your flesh,
Loving and caring in the world.

Prayers of Intercession

Leader: It is in this mystery of communion with Christ
That we pray for the Church throughout the world,
Praying in particular for . . . .
We are embodied with them, now.

We pray for the people and communities of faith
From whom we have come
and to whom we shall return . . . .
We are embodied with them, now.

We pray for the sick, the bereaved, the oppressed
And the homeless,
praying in particular for . . . .
We are embodied with them, now.

We pray for the broken and torn fabric of the earth
As it yearns for healing,
praying in particular for . . . .
We are embodied with Christ in creation, now.

And because you are one with us, O Christ,
Enable us to share your life with the world by
Sharing our own lives with the world,
And teach us now to pray together,
Our Father in heaven, ...

The Sharing of the Bread and Wine

Leader: Look,
The Body of Christ is broken
For the life of the world.
Here is Christ coming to us in bread and in wine.
The gifts of God
For the people of God.

The Sign of Peace

Leader: Many grains were gathered together to make this bread,
Many grapes were mixed to make this wine.
So we who are many,
And come from many places,
Are one in Christ.
May the peace of Christ be with you.

ALL: AND ALSO WITH YOU.

Leader: Let us greet one another with a sign of peace.

APPENDIX TO THE SERVICE OF WELCOME

Scripture Readings

(Words from Jesus concerning welcome, such as Matthew 10: 40-42, or stories of welcome and acceptance in Jesus' life and elsewhere in the scriptures, such as Genesis 18: 1-14)

A Sign of Welcome

Leader: May Christ be in our midst tonight and throughout the week. Let us greet one another with a word of welcome.

Prayer

Leader: O Christ, we bow before you in this shelter-house of prayer once more to give thanks.

Together we gather, celebrating your presence in creation around us, in the flowing air, in the fertile earth, and in the swift running tides of Iona.

Together we gather, glad of these strong walls which have given refuge to the broken and the poor through the centuries, aware of the countless prayers of joy and of suffering that have been uttered in this place.

O Christ, you have inspired the journeying of your people from all over the world to this island of sanctuary and light. Grace us with your continued presence and inspire us to be a people of hospitality.

Christ, in your mercy,

ALL: HEAR OUR PRAYER.

Leader: O Jesus, you sat at table with the betrayed and rejected of Palestine, we pray for those today who do not feel welcomed in their daily lives.

Christ, in your mercy,

ALL: HEAR OUR PRAYER.

Leader: O Jesus, you identified with the naked and with those who had no place to lay their heads. We pray for the thousands of homeless men and women, old and young, in our cities.

Christ, in your mercy,

ALL: HEAR OUR PRAYER.

Leader: O Jesus, you belonged to a refugee family. We pray for the millions of displaced people in our world, and for the opening of borders to the nationless.

Christ, in your mercy,

ALL: HEAR OUR PRAYER.

Leader: O Jesus, you cared for your companions and for the little ones who surrounded you. We pray for the ones whom we have left behind in coming to Iona, for the dependant ones whom God has given us to care for.

Christ, in your mercy,

ALL: HEAR OUR PRAYER.

Leader: O Jesus, you prayed that we might be one as you and the Father are one. We pray that during this week we may feel at home with one another and with you in our midst.

Christ, in your mercy,

ALL: HEAR OUR PRAYER.

Leader: And teach us now, O Christ, to pray as brothers and sisters . . .

ALL: 'OUR FATHER . . . '

Closing Prayer and Blessing

Leader: Stay with us Lord, since the day is far spent and the night is coming; kindle our hearts on the way, that we may recognise you in the scriptures, in the breaking of the bread, and in each other, for you live and guide us for ever.

ALL: AMEN.

Leader: And now may the grace of Jesus Christ, the love of God, And the communion of the Holy Spirit be with us all, This night and always.

ALL: AMEN.

APPENDIX FOR THE SERVICE OF PRAYER FOR JUSTICE AND PEACE

Chants

Freedom Is Coming (South Africa)
Senzenina (What have we done; South Africa)
Stand Firm (Cameroons)
Dona Nobis Pacem In Terra (Give us peace on earth)
Through Our Lives and By Our Prayers
The Lord Is My True Salvation
Kindle A Flame
Kyrie Eleison (U.S.S.R. or Ghana)

Songs

Sent By The Lord Am I (Nicaragua)
The Lord Is My Light (Czechoslovakia)
Jesus Christ Is Waiting
O Lord My God
Inspired By Love And Anger
From Each One Condemned By Birth
O Lord Hold My Hand
The Spirit Is Moving In My Heart
Do Not Retreat
Charity
Heiwa Song
The Love Burning Deep
Liberator Lord
Song For Love
Gather Us In

Scripture Readings

Old Testament: Gen 9: 8-17;   Deut 30: 6-8, 11-15;   1 Sam 2: 1-10;
Ps 9; 10; 51; 72: 1-15; 96; 97; 98; 113; 140: 1-8, 12-13;
Isa 2: 1-5; 55: 6-13; 58: 1-12; 61: 1-4; 63: 15-17;
Jer 31: 31-34;   Hosea 11: 1-10;   Micah 4: 1-4; 6: 1-3, 6-8;
Amos 5: 7, 10-24;   Malachi 3: 1-5.

New Testament: Mt 5: 1-12; 16: 24-26; 28: 1-10;
         Mk 1: 14-15;   Lk 4: 16-30; 6: 20-36; 12: 13-21, 32-34; 18: 18-29;
         Jn 20: 19-22; 20: 24-29;   Acts 4: 32-36;   1 Pet 3: 8-17;
         James 2: 1-5; 5: 1-6;   Eph 2: 13-22;   Gal 6: 1-5;   2 Cor 8: 1-9.

Alternative Affirmation (South Africa)

Leader: It is not true that this world and its inhabitants are doomed to die and be lost;

ALL: THIS IS TRUE: FOR GOD SO LOVED THE WORLD THAT HE GAVE HIS ONLY SON SO THAT EVERYONE WHO BELIEVES IN HIM SHALL NOT DIE BUT HAVE EVERLASTING LIFE.

Leader: It is not true that we must accept inhumanity and discrimination, hunger and poverty, death and destruction;

ALL: THIS IS TRUE: I HAVE COME THAT THEY MAY HAVE LIFE, AND HAVE IT ABUNDANTLY.

Leader: It is not true that violence and hatred shall have the last word, and that war and destruction have come to stay forever;

ALL: THIS IS TRUE: FOR TO US A CHILD IS BORN, TO US A SON IS GIVEN IN WHOM AUTHORITY WILL REST AND WHOSE NAME WILL BE PRINCE OF PEACE.

Leader: It is not true that we are simply victims of the powers of evil that seek to rule the world;

ALL: THIS IS TRUE: TO ME IS GIVEN ALL AUTHORITY IN HEAVEN AND ON EARTH, AND LO, I AM WITH YOU ALWAYS TO THE END OF THE WORLD.

Leader: It is not true that we have to wait for those who are specially gifted, who are the prophets of the church, before we can do anything;

ALL: THIS IS TRUE: I WILL POUR OUT MY SPIRIT ON ALL PEOPLE, AND YOUR SONS AND DAUGHTERS SHALL PROPHESY, YOUR YOUNG PEOPLE SHALL SEE VISIONS, AND YOUR OLD FOLK SHALL DREAM DREAMS.

Leader: It is not true that our dreams for the liberation of humankind, our dreams of justice, of human dignity, of peace, are not meant for this earth and this history;

ALL: THIS IS TRUE: THE HOUR COMES, AND IT IS NOW, THAT TRUE WORSHIPPERS SHALL WORSHIP GOD IN SPIRIT AND IN TRUTH.

Prayers of Confession

1.   O God, you are always true to us in love
And we are left wanting to say sorry
For our faithlessness to you and to one another,
For our forgetting of the poor and the broken,
For our failure to cherish creation.
Give us life, O God, to change
And enable us to change, that we may live.

2.   O God, gladly we live and move and have our being in you.
Yet always in the midst of this creation-glory,
We see sin's shadow and feel death's darkness:
Around us in the earth, sea and sky, the abuse of matter;
Beside us in the broken, the hungry and the poor,
The betrayal of one another;
And often, deep within us, a striving against your Spirit.
O Trinity of love,
Forgive us that we may forgive one another,
Heal us that we may be people of healing,
And renew us that we also may be makers of peace.

Prayers of Concern

1.   O God of all creation
Who has come to us in Jesus,
Lead us in your way of love
And fill us with your Spirit.
Choose us
To bring good news to the poor,
To proclaim liberty to the captives,
To bring sight to the blind
And set free the oppressed.
So shall your new creation come
And your will be done.
Amen.

2.   Spirit of truth and judgement,
Who alone can cast out
The powers that grip our world
At the point of crisis,
Give us your discernment,
That we may accurately name what is evil,
And know the way that leads to peace,
Through Jesus Christ,
Amen.

3.   Spirit of integrity,
You drive us into the desert
To search out our truth.
Give us clarity to know what is right,
That we may abandon the false innocence
Of failing to choose at all,
But may follow the purposes of Jesus Christ.
Amen.

4.   God of history,
You share our joys and crushing sorrows,
You hear the cries of the afflicted,
You fill the hungry,
And you set free the oppressed.
We pray for the end to all injustice.
Inspire us with the all-embracing love of God,
Challenge us with the sacrificial love of Jesus,
Empower us with the transforming love of the Spirit,
That we and all God's people may live and be free!
Amen.

5.   *(This prayer may be read by three voices)*

O God, the source of our being
And the goal of all our longing,
We believe and trust in you.
The whole earth is alive with your glory,
And all that has life is sustained by you.
Help us to commit ourselves to cherish your world,
And to seek your face.

O God, embodied in a human life,
We believe and trust in you.
Jesus our brother, born of the woman Mary,
You confronted the proud and the powerful,
And welcomed as your friends
Those of no account.
Holy Wisdom of God, firstborn of creation,
You emptied yourself of power,
And became foolishness for our sake.
You laboured with us upon the cross,
And have brought us forth
To the hope of resurrection.
Help us to commit ourselves to struggle against evil
And to choose life.

O God, life-giving Spirit,
Spirit of healing and comfort,
Of integrity and truth,
We believe and trust in you.
Warm-winged Spirit, brooding over creation,
Rushing wind and Pentecostal fire,
Help us to commit ourselves to work with you
And renew our world.

Blessing

May the God who shakes heaven and earth,
Whom death could not contain,
Who lives to disturb and heal us,
Bless you with power to go forth
And proclaim the gospel.
Amen.

APPENDIX FOR THE SERVICE OF PRAYER FOR HEALING

Welcome

*(As part of the welcome it is helpful to **very briefly** explain to people the shape of the service as outlined in 'Concerning Prayer for Healing' (p.36) with particular reference to the opportunity of receiving prayer and the laying on of hands in the second half of the service.)*

Scripture Reading

(Stories of healing from Jesus' life, such as Mark 1: 29-45, as well as Psalms and other passages imploring God's aid, such as Psalm 42, are helpful readings to include in the service.)

Songs

We Lay Our Broken World
Stumbling Blocks And Stepping Stones
Thirsting For God
A Touching Place
Take This Moment
We Cannot Measure How You Heal
The Lord Is My Light

Chants *(to be used as response to the readings or to the prayers of intercession)*

Nada Te Turbe (Let nothing worry you)
Kyrie Eleison (Lord have mercy)
Jesu Christe Miserere (Jesus Christ have mercy)
Stay With Me
O Lord Hear My Prayer
Bless The Lord My Soul
Lord Jesus Christ, Lover Of All

Prayers of Intercession

O Brother Jesus, you who walk with
the wounded along the road of our
world's suffering, we seek your grace
of healing for the broken people and
places of our world.

(followed by the lists of intercession.
It is best to have someone else assisting
in the prayers of intercession and also
in the prayers for the laying on of hands.)

The Invitation   *(the following words may be used)*

At the end of the next song those who seek prayer, either for
personal need or for a need in our world, are invited to come
and take it in turn to kneel or take a place at one of the
cushions here in the crossing.

Also those who wish to share in the laying on of hands may
come and simply place a hand on the shoulder or the arm of
the person in front of or next to them.

Those who wish to remain seated are invited to join in the first
prayer (or the second set of prayers) for the laying on of hands
on p.39.

Jesus says, 'Come to me all you who are troubled and I will
give you rest'.

So come, you who are burdened by regrets and anxieties,
You who are broken in body or in spirit,
You who are torn by relationships and by doubt,
You who feel deeply within yourselves the divisions and
injustices of our world.

Come, for Jesus invites us to bring him our brokenness.

Our song is . . .

Prayer for the Laying on of Hands

O great God, grant us your light.
O great God, grant us your grace.
O great God, grant us your joy
And let us be made pure in the well of your health.

(and then proceed to use either the first prayer or the second set
of prayers for the laying on of hands)

Closing Prayer and Benediction

Watch now, dear Lord, with those who wake
or watch or weep tonight, and give your angels
charge over those who sleep. Tend your
sick ones, O Lord Christ, rest your weary ones,
bless your dying ones, soothe your suffering
ones, pity your afflicted ones, shield
your joyous ones, and all for your love's sake.
Amen.

And now may the God of hope fill us with
all joy and peace in believing, that we may
abound in hope in the power of the
Holy Spirit.
Amen.

APPENDIX FOR THE CREATION LITURGY

Opening Responses *(alternative)*

Leader: Let the darkness of night surround us,
Let light and warmth gather us
And let God's people say Amen.

ALL: AMEN.

Leader: Let the tools be stored away,
Let the work be over and done
And let God's people say Amen.

ALL: AMEN.

Leader: Let the winds blow wild around us,
But let hearts be glad and minds be calm
And let God's people say Amen.

ALL: AMEN.

Songs

Many And Great (Native Indian Tradition)
You Are Author And Lord Of Creation (Sara Shriste; Nepal)
The Song Is Love
Sing Praise To God
Blessing And Honour
From Creation's Start
I Am For You
Lord Your Hands (Philippines)
Sing Out, Earth And Skies

Readings (Scriptures)

Psalms 19: 1-6; 23: 1-6; 29: 1-11; 46: 2-11; 65: 6-14; 67: 2-8;
72: 1-19; 80: 2-20; 84: 2-13; 85: 2-14; 89: 2-17; 96: 1-13;
97: 1-12; 100: 1-5; 104: 1-35; 131: 1-3; 147: 1-11; 148: 1-14.
Wisdom 7: 22-30. Job 38 & 39   Ecclesiasticus 42: 15-26; 43: 1-28.
Colossians 1: 15-20; 3: 11. Ephesians 1: 17-23.   Romans 8: 18-25.

Readings *(Mystics)*

A] *From:*   *Meditations with Hildegard of Bingen*

> The earth is at the same time mother,
> She is mother of all that is natural,
> Mother of all that is human.
>
> She is mother of all,
> For contained in her are the seeds of all.
>
> The earth of humankind contains all moistness,
> All verdancy,
> All germinating power.
>
> It is in so many ways fruitful.
>
> All creation comes from it
> Yet it forms not only the basic raw material for humankind,
> But also the substance of the incarnation of God's Son.

B] *From:*   *Meditations with Julian of Norwich*

> I saw that God was everything that is good
> And encouraging.
>
> God is our clothing
> That wraps, clasps and encloses us
> So as never to leave us.
>
> God showed me in my palm
> A little thing round as a ball
> About the size of a hazelnut.
>
> I looked at it with the eye of my understanding
> And asked myself:
> "What is this thing?"
> And I was answered: "It is everything that is created."
>
> I wondered how it could survive since it seemed so little
> It could suddenly disintegrate into nothing.
>
> The answer came: "It endures and ever will endure,
> Because God loves it."
>
> And so everything has being because of God's love.

C] *From:*   *Meditations with Meister Eckhart*

> Apprehend God in all things,
> For God is in all things.
>
> Every single creature is full of God
> And is a book about God.

80

Every creature is a word of God.

If I spent enough time with the tiniest creature –
Even a caterpillar –
I would never have to prepare a sermon.
So full of God
Is every creature.

Prayers of Intercession

Prayer of Intercession based on Colossians 1: 15-20.

O Christ, your cross speaks both to us and to our world.

In your dying for us you accepted the pain and hurt
Of the whole of creation.

The arms of your cross stretch out across the
Broken world in reconciliation.

You have made peace with us.
Help us to make peace with you by sharing in your
Reconciling work.

May we recognise your spirit disturbing and
Challenging us to care for creation and for the
Poor who most feel the effects of its abuse.

O Christ, the whole of creation groans,
Set us free and make us whole.

Prayer of Intercession based on Ephesians 4: 7-16.

There is no pain in our hearts or in our planet
That you do not know,
For you have touched the lowest places on earth.

Teach us to grieve with you, O Christ, the loss of
All the beauty that is being killed.

There is no place in the heavens that cannot be
Touched by your resurrection presence,
For you fill all things.

Give us strength in your victory over death
To grow into your way of love,
Which does not despair but keeps sowing seeds of hope
And making signs of wholeness.

Under Christ's control all the different parts of
The body fit together and the whole body is held
Together by every joint with which it is provided.

81

Teach us to know our interconnectedness
With all things.
Teach us to grow with each other
And all living creatures through love.

Actions

*Some actions may be better placed after the prayers of
intercessions as with the following examples:*

*— People to light candles around a cross to signify their share
in reconciling creation to God (Colossians 1: 15-20)*

*— People to add stones to a spiral of growth at the foot of a
cross committing themselves to growing in God's way of love
for creation and grieving the crucifixion of life on earth
(Ephesians 4: 7-16)*

Chants

Kindle A Flame
Dona Nobis Pacem In Terra (Give us peace on earth)
Kyrie Eleison (Lord have mercy: U.S.S.R. or Ghana)
Mayenziwe (Your will be done: South Africa)
Your Kingdom Come O Lord (U.S.S.R.)
Agios O Theos (Holy God have mercy: U.S.S.R.)
Come Holy Spirit

APPENDIX FOR THE SERVICE OF COMMITMENT

Welcome

*(As part of the welcome it is helpful to **very briefly** explain to the congregation the shape of the service as outlined in 'Concerning the Act of Commitment Service' (p. 42), with particular reference to the opportunity to make a sign of commitment in the service.)*

Scripture Reading

(Stories from Jesus' life in which he calls people to follow him, such as Matthew 19: 16-30, are helpful readings to make use of in this service.)

Songs

Come Take My Hand
The Summons
Sing Hey For The Carpenter
Lord Jesus Christ
Jesus Christ Is Waiting
The Spirit Is Moving In My Heart

Chants *(to be used as response to the readings or at other points in the service)*

Through Our Lives And By Our Prayers
Yesuve Saranam (Jesus I surrender)
Jesu Tawa Pano (Jesus, we are here for you)
Thuma Mina (Send me Jesus)
Sent By The Lord Am I

The Call To Commitment

(After briefly expanding on the Scripture Reading along the theme of commitment as outlined in 'Concerning the Act of Commitment Service' (p.42), the following words of invitation could be used.)

Come and follow Jesus,

You who have commited yourselves already,

And you who would like to do so for the first time;

You who have given yourselves to the care of creation
And to the suffering ones of the world,

And you who feel moved by the Spirit to begin to so offer
yourselves;

You who have been faithful in your life commitments

And you who have failed.

Come, for our Lord invites us to follow him,
And to make new beginnings in our lives.

There is opportunity at the end of the next song to make an outward sign of commitment by moving forward to the front of the church and, after affirming our faith, to kneel and receive the words and promises of Jesus.

Please bring your Worship Book with you.

Our song is . . .

An Alternative Affirmation Of Faith

Leader: Let us affirm our faith

ALL: WE BELIEVE IN GOD
WHOSE LOVE IS THE SOURCE OF ALL LIFE
AND THE DESIRE OF OUR LIVES,
WHOSE LOVE WAS GIVEN A HUMAN FACE
IN JESUS OF NAZARETH,
WHOSE LOVE WAS CRUCIFIED BY THE EVIL
THAT WAITS TO ENSLAVE US ALL
AND WHOSE LOVE, DEFEATING EVEN DEATH,
IS OUR GLORIOUS PROMISE OF FREEDOM.

THEREFORE, THOUGH WE ARE SOMETIMES FEARFUL
   AND FULL OF DOUBT,
   IN GOD WE TRUST;
AND, IN THE NAME OF JESUS CHRIST, WE COMMIT
   OURSELVES, IN THE SERVICE OF OTHERS,
   TO SEEK JUSTICE AND TO LIVE IN PEACE,
TO CARE FOR THE EARTH AND TO SHARE THE
   COMMONWEALTH OF GOD'S GOODNESS,
TO LIVE IN THE FREEDOM OF FORGIVENESS,
   AND THE POWER OF THE SPIRIT OF LOVE,
AND IN THE COMPANY OF THE FAITHFUL
   SO TO BE THE CHURCH,
FOR THE GLORY OF GOD.
AMEN.

Prayer   *(before the words of Jesus)*

O God of the high heavens,
O Christ of the deep earth,
O Spirit of the flowing waters,
O Trinity of love,
You have offered your love to us,
And here we pledge our love to you.

You have been faithful to your people through the ages,
And here we pledge our faithfulness to one another.

You have sustained in love the earth, sea and sky around us,
And here we pledge our sustaining love for creation.

You have identified with the powerless
and the weak of the world,
And here we pledge our identification with them.

O God, strengthen us in our desire,
And breathe into our bodies the passion of your love.
We pray this in the name of Jesus,
To whom we commit ourselves.
Amen.

The Words Of Jesus

(it is best to have someone else assisting in the saying of these words to provide a second voice)

Hear now the words of Jesus spoken to each one of us.

Jesus says:

My peace I give to you.

Do not be afraid.

I call you my friend.

Abide in my love.

Even the hairs of your head are numbered.

Follow me.

I am the way for you.

I am the life for you.

I am the truth for you.

Blessed are your eyes for they see.

You are my witness.

You are my brother.

I am hungry, give me food.

I am in prison, come to me.

I am thirsty, give me drink.

I am a stranger, welcome me.

I am naked, clothe me.

I am sick, visit me.

Abide in me and I in you.

I will drink wine with you in the Kingdom of God

You will shine like the sun.

You are in me and I in you.

Ask and it will be given you.

Seek and you will find.

Knock and the door will be opened to you.

I am the vine, you are the branch.

I will give you rest.

You are the light of the world.

You are the salt of the earth.

You are my sister.

Give and it will be given to you.

Love others as I have loved you.

The truth will make you free.

Feed my sheep.

Watch and pray.

I am with you always.

(Many other words of Jesus can be appropriately included, but it is advisable to keep to as simple a phrase as possible and to maintain direct speech in the sayings)

APPENDIX FOR AN EVENING SERVICE OF COMMUNION

Prayer of Invocation

Come Lord Jesus, be our guest,
Stay with us for day is ending.

With friend, with stranger,
With young and with old,
Be among us tonight.

Come close to us that we may come close to you.
Forgive us that we may forgive one another.
Renew us so that, where we have failed,
We may begin again.　　　　Amen.

Words of Invitation

At the Last Supper Jesus, sharing bread and wine,
Invited the disciples to share his journey.
Like many grains of wheat becoming one loaf of bread,
The disciples were invited to become one body with him.

Here tonight, through bread and wine,
We renew our journey with Jesus and his disciples.

Here, through bread and wine,
We renew our unity with one another,
And with all those who have gone before us in this place.

Through bread and wine,
We renew our communion with the earth
And our interwovenness with the broken ones of the world.

So come, taste of this bread and wine,
Gifts of the earth, work of human hands,
Food both of earth and of heaven.

The Lord be with you . . .

The Story of The Last Supper

Among friends, gathered round a table,
Jesus took bread,
And, having blessed it,
He broke the bread
And gave it to his disciples, saying,
'This is my body which is given for you'.

In the same way he took wine,
And, having given thanks for it,
He poured it out
And gave the cup to his disciples, saying,
'This cup is the new relationship with God,
 Sealed with my blood.
 Take this and share it.
 I shall drink wine with you next in the coming
      kingdom of God'.

So now, following Jesus' example,
We take this bread and this wine;
The ordinary things of the world through which God
      will bless us.
And, as Jesus offered thanks for the gifts of the earth,
Let us also celebrate God's goodness.

The Prayer of Thanksgiving

Blessed are you, O God,
For you have brought forth bread from the earth.
Blessed are you, O God,
For you have created the fruit of the vine.

In the beginning you watered the earth
That man and woman might have food and drink.

You gave to your servant Sarah
Bread to strengthen her family on their journey,
And wine to make them glad.

You called Moses and his people out of bondage
And refreshed them with food in the wilderness.

You gave Mary and Jesus their daily bread to share.

And here at your table
You offer us bread and wine for the journey
To nourish us as sons and daughters.

And so with all our sisters and brothers,
Before us and beside us,
We join in the song of your unending greatness.

The Blessing of the Bread and the Wine

Lord Jesus Christ,
Present with us now,
As we do in this place what you did in an upstairs room,
Breathe your Spirit upon us
And upon this bread and this wine,
That they may be heaven's food and drink for us,
Renewing, sustaining and making us whole,
And that we may be your body on earth,
Loving and caring in the world.

The Prayers of Intercession

You are above us, O God,
You are beneath.

You are in air, you are in earth,
You are beside us, you are within.

O God, you are in the betrayed and suffering people of
our world
Just as you were in the broken body of Jesus.

We pray now for all that concerns us as we sit at
table together.

Let us offer our own prayers
Both spoken and unspoken.

The Breaking and Sharing of the Bread and Wine

Look,
The Bread of Heaven is broken for the life of the world.

The gifts of God for the people of God.

Words at the Sign of peace

As this broken bread was scattered through fields and hills
before being gathered to become one,
So may we and all people be gathered from the ends of the
earth into Christ's kingdom.

May the peace of Christ be with you.
Let us greet one another with a sign of peace.

Songs

The Song Of The Supper
Come Lord Be Our Guest
God's Table
The Lord Of All
Love Is The Welcome
These I Lay Down
Among Us And Before Us
O Give Thanks To The Lord

Chants

We Come To Share Our Story
Holy, Holy (various)
We Sing Your Glory
Kyrie Eleison (various)
Jesu Christe Miserere

Recessional Chants

Alleluia (various)
We Are Marching
Amen Alleluia
Amen Siakudumisa
Sanna

APPENDIX OF GENERAL WORSHIP RESOURCES

RESPONSES AND PRAYERS

A. RESPONSES

In The Beginning

Leader: In the beginning,
When it was very dark,
God said, "Let there be light"

ALL: AND THERE WAS LIGHT.

*(The sign of light,
A lighted candle is placed on a central table)*

Leader: In the beginning,
When it was very quiet,
The Word was with God

ALL: AND WHAT GOD WAS, THE WORD WAS.

*(The sign of the Word,
An open bible is placed on the table)*

Leader: When the time was right
God sent the Son.

ALL: HE CAME AMONG US,
HE WAS ONE OF US.

*(The sign of the Son,
A cross is placed on the table)*

Hope For The World

Leader: In quietness and darkness,
In peace and confusion,
Jesus Christ wants to make his home
And meet his friends.
He is the light of life:

ALL: HE IS THE HOPE FOR THE WORLD.

Leader: In him there is neither Jew nor Gentile,
Neither Roman Catholic nor Protestant,

ALL: ALL ARE ONE IN JESUS CHRIST.

Leader: He is the light of life:

ALL: HE IS THE HOPE OF THE WORLD.

Leader: In him there is neither black nor white,
Neither north nor south:

ALL: ALL ARE ONE IN JESUS CHRIST.

Leader: He is the light of life:

ALL: HE IS THE HOPE OF THE WORLD.

Leader: In him there is neither male nor female,
Neither master nor servant:

ALL: ALL ARE ONE IN JESUS CHRIST.

Leader: He is the light of life:

ALL: HE IS THE HOPE FOR THE WORLD.

Leader: In him there is neither rich nor poor,
Neither middle class nor working class:

ALL: ALL ARE ONE IN JESUS CHRIST.

Leader: He is the light of life:

ALL: HE IS THE HOPE FOR THE WORLD.

Made In Love

Leader: In the beginning, God made the world,

ALL: MADE IN LOVE FOR MAN AND WOMAN;

Leader: The earth was filled with lovely things,

ALL: MADE IN LOVE FOR MAN AND WOMAN;

Leader: Out of the dust God made new creatures,

ALL: MADE IN LOVE FOR MAN AND WOMAN;

Leader: These, God said, were in God's image,

ALL: MADE IN LOVE FOR MAN AND WOMAN;

Leader: And to the world there came God's Son,

ALL: KING OF LOVE, FOR MAN AND WOMAN.

When The Lights Are On

Leader: When the lights are on
And the house is full
And laughter is easy
And all is well . . . .

Voice: Behold I stand at the door and knock.

Leader: When the lights are low
And the house is still
And the talk is intense
And the air is full of wondering . . . .

Voice: Behold I stand at the door and knock.

Leader: When the lights are off
And the house is sad
And the voice is troubled
And nothing seems right . . . .

Voice: Behold I stand at the door and knock.

Leader: And tonight
Always tonight,
As if there were no other people,
no other house,
no other door . . . .

Voice: Behold I stand at the door and knock.

Leader: Come, Lord Jesus, be our guest,
Stay with us for the day is ending.
Bring to our house your poverty,

ALL: FOR THEN SHALL WE BE RICH.

Leader: Bring to our house your pain,

ALL: THAT SHARING IT WE MAY ALSO SHARE YOUR JOY.

Leader: Bring to our house your understanding of us,

ALL: THAT WE MAY BE FREED TO LEARN MORE OF YOU.

Leader: Bring to our house all those
Who hurry or hirple (hobble) behind you,

ALL: THAT WE MAY MEET YOU AS THE SAVIOUR OF ALL.

Leader: Bring to our house your Holy Spirit,

ALL: THAT THIS MAY BE A CRADLE OF LOVE.

Leader: With friend, with stranger,
With neighbour, and the well-known ones,
Be among us tonight,

ALL: FOR THE DOORS OF OUR HOUSE WE OPEN
AND THE DOORS OF OUR HEARTS WE LEAVE AJAR.

O Come, Let Us Worship

ALL: O COME, LET US WORSHIP AND BOW DOWN,
            LET US KNEEL BEFORE THE LORD OUR MAKER,
            FOR GOD IT IS WHO MADE US,
            NOT WE OURSELVES.

A: Womb, dark and lifeless,
            You knitted us with love.

B: Growing and grappling,
            You grasped us with love.

A: Wandering and doubtful,
            You held us with love.

B: Suffering and sickened,
            You healed us with love.

A: Searching uncertainly,
            You found us with love.

B: And in the following
            You lead us with love.

ALL: TODAY, TOMORROW AND ALWAYS.

The Sun Rises

Leader: The sun rises and it is light, night falls and it is dark.
ALL: BLESS THE ONE WHO GIVES THE LIFE.
Men: Sow the seed and cut the corn;
Women: Bear the child and build the house;
ALL: BLESS THE ONE WHO GIVES THE LIFE.
Men: Lay the stone and light the fire;
Women: Cast the net and water the earth;
ALL: BLESS THE ONE WHO GIVES THE LIFE.
Men: Serve the guest and pay the price;
Women: Nail the wood and pick the flowers;
ALL: BLESS THE ONE WHO GIVES THE LIFE.
Men: Make the wine and bake the bread;
Women: Pour the wine and break the bread;
ALL: BLESS THE ONE WHO GIVES THE LIFE.

Witnesses For Peace

Leader: Sisters and brothers in Jesus Christ,
Let us call to mind and to be present with us
Those who have lived, worked, spoken and witnessed for peace
In this and other ages.
Jesus Christ, Prince of Peace . . . .

ALL: STAND WITH US NOW.

Leader: Mary Magdalene, witness to the resurrection . . . .

ALL: STAND WITH US NOW.

Leader: Paul of Tarsus, Apostle of Peace . . . .

ALL: STAND WITH US NOW.

(At this point, throughout the Abbey, people may mention a name or names of those who have inspired them on issues of justice and peace. After stating the name, they say, "STAND WITH US NOW". They rise on speaking and others around them who want to be associated with that name, stand also e.g. "Francis of Assisi . . . . STAND WITH US NOW".)

After names have been called, the leader will proceed:

Leader: All you who have died in war
Since the war to end all wars . . . .

ALL: STAND WITH US NOW.

Leader: All you who tread the path of peace . . . .

ALL: STAND WITH US NOW.

Leader: Sisters and brothers in Jesus Christ,
Let us stand in silence,
For the world is worried
And the Prince of Peace is moving towards a cross.

(Silence)

Leader: Do not be afraid . . . . says Jesus,
I have overcome the world.
The peace I give, the world will never take away.

We Call On The Power Of God

Leader: We call on the power of God to meet us in our helplessness:

ALL: GOD IN OUR THINKING, GOD IN OUR SPEAKING.

Leader: We call on the clarity of God to meet us in our confusion:

ALL: GOD IN OUR ACTING, GOD IN OUR STILLNESS.

Leader: We call on the mercy of God to meet us in our brokenness:

ALL: GOD IN OUR WAKING, GOD IN OUR SLEEPING.

Leader: We call on the Spirit of God to meet us in our division:

ALL: GOD IN OUR MEETING, GOD IN OUR PARTING.

The Kingdom Of God

Power to Choose

Leader: Out of the darkness came light
ALL: AND THE POWER OF GOD WAS REVEALED:
Men: In the running wave and the flowing air,
Women: In the quiet earth and the shining stars.
Leader: Out of the dust came life
ALL: AND THE IMAGE OF GOD WAS REVEALED:
Men: In the human face and the gentle heart,
Women: In the warmth of flesh and the depth of soul.
Leader: Out of justice came freedom
ALL: AND THE WISDOM OF GOD WAS REVEALED:
Men: In the need to grow and the will to love,
Women: In the chance to know and the power to choose.
Leader: And God looked at the creation
ALL: AND BEHOLD IT WAS VERY GOOD.

Power to Change

Leader: Out of judgement came mercy
ALL: AND GOD DID NOT ABANDON THE PEOPLE,
Men: For the love that God bore them, coming again,
Women: For the hope that God had for them, bearing their pain.
Leader: Out of gentleness came strength
ALL: AND GOD SPOKE A WORD:
Men: To the outcast and stranger, making them welcome,
Women: To the sick and despairing, making them whole.
Leader: Out of freedom came faithfulness
ALL: AND GOD DIED ON THE CROSS:
Men: For the poor and the prisoner, the sign of deliverance;
Women: For God loved the world so much that he gave his only Son
ALL: THAT EVERYONE WHO BELIEVES IN HIM MAY NOT DIE, BUT HAVE ETERNAL LIFE.

Power to Love

Leader: Out of death came life

ALL: AND GOD DEFEATED EVIL:

Men: An empty cross and an empty tomb,

Women: A nail mark shown and a presence known.

Leader: Out of sorrow came joy

ALL: AND GOD SENT THE SPIRIT:

Men: Coming like fire to all people and ages,

Women: Coming to birth in the water of life.

Leader: Out of difference came unity

ALL: AND GOD'S PEOPLE WERE CALLED:

Men: Called to receive him in bread and wine,

Women: Called to be free in the power of love.

Leader: For when the Holy Spirit comes upon you,
You will be filled with power

ALL: AND BE WITNESSES FOR CHRIST TO THE ENDS OF THE
EARTH.

God's Power Shown

Leader: Out of love comes celebration

ALL: AND GOD'S KINGDOM IS AMONG US:

Men: Where peace is the means of making us one,

Women: Where truth does not stumble and justice is done.

Leader: Out of change comes possibility

ALL: AND GOD'S NEW CREATION IS BEGUN:

Men: Promise of splendour and signal of worth,

Women: Source of all goodness, renewing the earth.

Leader: Out of freedom comes responsibility

ALL: AND GOD CALLS US TO DISCIPLESHIP:

Men: In our compassion, making love known,

Women: In our conviction, God's power shown.

Leader: You did not choose me, I chose you.

ALL: THIS, THEN, IS WHAT I COMMAND YOU: LOVE ONE ANOTHER.

Blessing The World

Leader: People of Ireland,
    torn and tired of being torn . . . .

ALL: GOD'S PEACE IS FOR YOU.

Leader: People of Africa,
    exploited and tired of being exploited . . . .

ALL: GOD'S PEACE IS FOR YOU.

Leader: People of the Middle East,
    turbulent and tired of being turbulent . . . .

ALL: GOD'S PEACE IS FOR YOU

Leader: People of South America,
    silenced and tired of being silenced . . . .

ALL: GOD'S PEACE IS FOR YOU.

Leader: People of India,
    divided and tired of being divided . . . .

ALL: GOD'S PEACE IS FOR YOU.

Leader: People of Eastern Europe,
    anxious and tired of being anxious . . . .

ALL: GOD'S PEACE IS FOR YOU.

Leader: People of the West,
    privileged and tired of being privileged . . . .

ALL: GOD'S PEACE IS FOR YOU.

Leader: May the God of all people and the Lord Jesus Christ
    give us grace and peace this night and every night.

ALL: AMEN.

God Of Life

Leader: O God of life, of all life and of each life,
    We lay our lives before you.
    We give our lives to you, from whom nothing in us is hidden.

Women: You are before us, God, you are behind;

Men: You are around us, God, you are within.

Leader: O God of life, you know the secret thoughts of every heart.

Women: We bring the faith that is in us, and the doubt;

Men: We bring the joy that is in us, and the sorrow.

Leader: O God of life, you are in the light, and in the darkness.

Women: We bring the knowledge that is in us, and the ignorance;

Men: We bring the hope that is in us, and the despair.

Leader: O God of life, O generous Spirit,

ALL: RENEW US WITH YOUR LIFE,
    TONIGHT, TOMORROW AND ALWAYS.   AMEN.

We Are Not Alone

Leader: We are not alone.
We live in God's world;

ALL: WE BELIEVE IN GOD,
WHO HAS CREATED AND IS CREATING,
WHO HAS COME IN JESUS TO RECONCILE
AND TO MAKE ALL THINGS NEW.
WE TRUST GOD,
WHO CALLS US TO BE THE CHURCH;
TO LOVE AND SERVE OTHERS,
TO SEEK JUSTICE AND TO RESIST EVIL,
TO PROCLAIM JESUS,
CRUCIFIED, DEAD AND RISEN;
OUR JUDGE AND OUR HOPE.
IN LIFE,
IN DEATH,
IN LIFE BEYOND DEATH,
GOD IS WITH US:
WE ARE NOT ALONE.
THANKS BE TO GOD.

The Cross

Leader: The cross . . . .

ALL: WE SHALL TAKE IT.

Leader: The bread . . . .

ALL: WE SHALL BREAK IT.

Leader: The pain . . . .

ALL: WE SHALL BEAR IT.

Leader: The joy . . . .

ALL: WE SHALL SHARE IT.

Leader: The gospel . . . .

ALL: WE SHALL LIVE IT.

Leader: The love . . . .

ALL: WE SHALL GIVE IT.

Leader: The light . . . .

ALL: WE SHALL CHERISH IT.

Leader: The darkness . . . .

ALL: GOD SHALL PERISH IT.
AMEN.

B. PRAYERS
Make Us One

Leader: O Trinity of love,
One God,
In perfect community,
Look now on us
Who look to you . . . .

ALL: AND HEAR OUR PRAYER FOR OUR COMMUNITY:

Leader: Where there is falseness . . . .

ALL: SMOTHER IT BY YOUR TRUTH;

Leader: Where there is any coldness . . . .

ALL: KINDLE THE FLAME OF YOUR LOVE;

Leader: Where there is joy and hope . . . .

ALL: FREE US TO SHARE IT TOGETHER;

Leader: And make us one . . . .

ALL: AS YOU ARE ONE.

Leader: Before God and you who are near me,
I release anything I hold against you;
I regret all I have done to harm you;
I stand beside the wrong in my life
And ask for God's forgiveness.

ALL: BEFORE GOD AND YOU WHO ARE NEAR,
WE RELEASE ANYTHING WE HOLD AGAINST ONE ANOTHER;
WE REGRET ALL THE HARM WE HAVE DONE;
WE STAND BESIDE THE WRONG IN OUR LIVES
AND ASK FOR GOD'S FORGIVENESS.

(Silence)

Leader: Jesus says to us, each one:
'Go and sin no more,
Come and follow me'.
Now bind our hands with honesty
As we offer them to each other
And our prayer to you: − *(join hands if appropriate)*

ALL: OUR FATHER IN HEAVEN,
HALLOWED BE YOUR NAME;
YOUR KINGDOM COME, YOUR WILL BE DONE,
ON EARTH AS IT IS IN HEAVEN.
GIVE US TODAY OUR DAILY BREAD.
FORGIVE US OUR SINS
AS WE FORGIVE THOSE WHO SIN AGAINST US.
SAVE US FROM THE TIME OF TRIAL
AND DELIVER US FROM EVIL.
FOR THE KINGDOM, THE POWER AND THE GLORY ARE YOURS,
NOW AND FOR EVER.   AMEN.

Prayer Of Adoration And Confession

Leader: Let us pray.
O God,
Early in the morning,
When the world was young,
You made life in all its beauty and terror;
You gave birth to all that we know.

ALL: HALLOWED BE YOUR NAME.

Leader: Early in the morning,
When the world least expected it,
A new born child crying in a cradle
Announced that you had come among us,
That you were one of us.

ALL: HALLOWED BE YOUR NAME.

Leader: Early in the morning,
Surrounded by self-interested religious leaders,
Anxious statesmen
And silent friends,
You accepted the penalty for doing good,
for being God:
You shouldered and suffered the cross.

ALL: HALLOWED BE YOUR NAME.

Leader: Early in the morning,
A voice in a guarded graveyard
And footsteps in the dew
Proved that you had risen,
that you had come back
To those and for those
Who had forgotten, denied and destroyed you.

ALL: O GOD, BRING NEW LIFE,
WHERE WE ARE WORN AND TIRED,
NEW LOVE,
WHERE WE HAVE TURNED HARD HEARTED,
FORGIVENESS,
WHERE WE HAVE WOUNDED,
AND THE JOY AND FREEDOM OF YOUR HOLY SPIRIT,
WHERE WE ARE THE PRISONERS OF OUR SELVES.

(Silence)

Leader: To all and to each,
Where regret is real,
God pronounces pardon
And grants us the right to begin again.
Thanks be to God!

The Gospel Of The God Of Life

The gospel of the God of life to shelter us:
The gospel of the God of life to help us,
To keep us from all malice, to keep us from all anguish.
Christ himself is shepherd over us,
Enfolding us on every side.
He will not leave us forsaken, nor let evil come near us.

May God's Goodness Be Yours

May God's goodness be yours,
And well, and seven times well, may you spend your lives:
May you be an isle in the sea,
May you be a hill on the shore,
May you be a star in the darkness,
May you be a staff to the weak;
May the love Christ Jesus gave fill every heart for you;
May the love Christ Jesus gave fill you for every one.

The Blessing Of The God Of Life

The blessing of the God of life be ours,
The blessing of the loving Christ be ours,
The blessing of the Holy Spirit be ours,
To cherish us, to help us, to make us holy.

God Of Life, Do Not Darken Your Light

God of life, do not darken your light to us,
O God of life, do not close your joy to us,
O God of life, do not shut your door to us,
O God of life, do not refuse your mercy to us,
And, O God of life, crown us with your gladness.

Christ Stands Before You

Christ stands before you, and peace is in his mind.
Sleep in the calm of all calm,
Sleep in the guidance of all guidance,
Sleep in the love of all loves:
Sleep, beloved, in the God of life.

O God, Give Us Your Shielding

O God, give us your shielding,
O God, give us your holiness,
O God, give us your comfort
And your peace at the hour of our death.

O God, Our Creator

O God, our Creator,
Your kindness has brought us the gift of a new day.
Help us to leave yesterday,
And not to covet tomorrow,
But to accept the uniqueness of today.

O God, Open To Us Today

O God, open to us today the sea of your mercy
And water us with full streams
From the riches of your grace
And springs of your kindness.
Make us children of quietness and heirs of peace:
Kindle in us the fire of your love;
Sow in us your fear;
Strengthen our weakness by your power
And bind us close to you and to each other.

Lord, Set Your Blessing On Us

Lord, set your blessing on us
As we begin this day together.
Confirm in us the truth by which we rightly live;
Confront us with the truth from which we wrongly turn.
We ask not for what we want,
But for what you know we need,
As we offer this day and ourselves for you and to you,
Through Jesus Christ, our Saviour.

O My Soul's Healer

O my souls' healer, keep me at evening;
Keep me at morning, keep me at noon.
I am tired, astray and stumbling,
Shield me from sin.

My Christ, My Shield

My Christ, my shield, my encircler,
Each day, each night, each light, each dark,
Be near me, uphold me, my treasure, my triumph.

God To Enfold Us

God to enfold us, God to surround us;
God in our speaking, God in our thinking;
God in our life, God on our lips;
God in our souls, God in our hearts.

Peace Between Neighbours

Peace between neighbours;
Peace between kindred;
Peace between lovers
In love of the God of life.

PSALM APPENDIX

Psalms In A Five Week Cycle

Weeks		I	II	III	IV	V
Monday	(Justice and Peace Themes)	10	72	82	139	146
Tuesday	(Healing Themes)	42	46	103	130	142
Wednesday	(Creation Themes)	8	19	29	93	148
Thursday	(Commitment Themes)	27	33	40	98	116
Friday	(Communion Themes)	16	23	96	126	133
Saturday	(General Themes)	24	100	113	121	138

APPENDIX OF PSALMS

Psalm 8

ALL: O GOD, OUR GOD,
HOW GLORIOUS IS YOUR NAME OVER ALL THE EARTH!
YOUR GLORY IS PRAISED IN THE HEAVENS.

A: Out of the mouths of children and babes
you have fashioned praise because of your foes,
to silence the enemy and the rebellious.

B: When I look at your heavens, the work of your hands,
the moon and the stars which you created −

A: Who are we that you should be mindful of us,
that you should care for us?

B: You have made us little less than the gods
and crowned us with glory and honour.

A: You have given us rule over the works of your hands,
putting all things under our feet:

B: All sheep and oxen,
yes, and the beasts of the field;

A: The birds of the air, the fishes of the sea,
and whatever swims the paths of the seas.

ALL: GOD, OUR GOD,
HOW GLORIOUS IS YOUR NAME OVER ALL THE EARTH!
AMEN.

Psalm 10

A: Why do you stand aloof, O God?
    Why do you hide yourself in times of trouble?

B: In arrogance the wicked oppress the poor
    who are caught in the schemes
    that the wicked have devised.

A: For the wicked boast of their hearts' desires,
    and those greedy for gain curse and renounce you.

B: The wicked do not seek you, because of their pride;
    All their thoughts are, "There is no God".

A: The ways of the wicked prosper at all times;
    your judgements are on high, out of their sight.
    As for all their foes, they scorn them.

B: They think in their hearts, "We shall not be moved;
    throughout all generations we shall not meet adversity".

A: Their mouths are filled with cursing, deceit and oppression;
    under their tongues are mischief and fraud.

B: They lurk in ambush in the villages;
    in hiding places they murder the innocent;
    their eyes stealthily watch for the helpless.

A: They lie in wait that they may seize the poor;
    they catch the afflicted and draw them into their net.

B: The helpless are crushed, sink down,
    and fall by their might.

A: Arise, Yahweh! O God, lift up your hand!
    Forget not the afflicted!

B: You do see; yes, you behold misery and sorrow,
    taking them into your hands.
    The helpless commit themselves to you,
    you have been the helper of the orphan.

A: Break the strength of the wicked and evildoer;
    seek out wickedness till you find none.

B: Yahweh, you will hear the desire of the afflicted;
    you will strengthen their hearts;

A: You will incline your ear to do justice to the orphan and the
    oppressed, so that those born of earth may strike terror no more.

ALL: AMEN.

Psalm 16

A: Protect me, God, because I come to you for safety.

B: I say, "You are my God;
    all the good things I have come from you".

A: How wonderful are your faithful people!
    My greatest pleasure is to be with them.

B: Those who rush to other gods
bring trouble on themselves.
I will not take part in their sacrifices;
I will not worship their gods.

A: You, Yahweh, are all I have,
and you give me all I need: my life is in your hands.

B: How wonderful are your gifts to me;
how good they are!

A: I praise Yahweh, who guides me,
and in the night my conscience teaches me.

B: I am always aware of your presence;
you are near, and nothing can shake me.

A: And so I am full of happiness and joy,
and I always feel secure.

B: Because you will not allow me
to go to the world of the dead;
you will not abandon to the depths below
the one you love.

A: You will show me the path that leads to life;
your presence fills me with joy,
and your help brings pleasure forever.

ALL: AMEN.

Psalm 19

ALL: THE HEAVENS PROCLAIM YOUR GLORY, O GOD,
AND THE FIRMAMENT SHOWS FORTH
THE WORK OF YOUR HANDS.

A: Day carries the news to day
and night brings the message to night.

B: No speech, no word,
no voice is heard;

A: Yet their news goes forth through all the earth,
their words to the farthest bounds of the world.
There you pitched a tent for the sun;

B: It comes forth like a bridegroom from his tent,
like a champion eager to run the race.

A: At the end of the sky is the rising of the sun;
the boundary of the sky is its course.
There is nothing hidden from its scorching heat.

B: Your law, Yahweh, is perfect,
it refreshes the soul.
Your rule is to be trusted,
it gives wisdom to the simple.

A: Your precepts, Yahweh, are right,
they gladden the heart.
Your command is clear,
it gives light to the eyes.

B: Fear of you, Yahweh, is holy,
abiding for ever.
Your decrees are faithful,
and all of them just.

A: They are more desirable than gold,
than the purest of gold,
and sweeter than honey are they,
than honey oozing from the comb.

B: So in them your servant finds instruction;
in keeping them is great reward.

A: But who can detect failings?
From hidden faults forgive me.

B: From presumption restrain your servant,
and let it not rule me.
Then I shall be blameless,
free from grave sin.

ALL: MAY THE SPOKEN WORDS OF MY MOUTH,
THE THOUGHTS OF MY HEART,
WIN FAVOUR IN YOUR SIGHT, O YAHWEH,
MY REDEEMER. MY ROCK! AMEN.

Psalm 23

A: Yahweh, you are my shepherd;
I shall not want.

B: In verdant pastures you give me repose.
Beside restful waters you lead me;

A: You refresh my soul.
You guide me in right paths
for your name's sake.

B: Even though I walk in the dark valley
I fear no evil;
for you are at my side.
Your rod and your staff give me courage.

A: You spread the table before me
in the sight of my foes.
You anoint my head with oil;
my cup brims over.

B: Only goodness and kindness follow me
all the days of my life;
and I shall dwell in your house
for years to come.

ALL: AMEN.

Psalm 24

ALL: THE WORLD AND ALL THAT IS IN IT BELONG TO YAHWEH,
THE EARTH AND ALL WHO LIVE IN IT.

A: Yahweh built it on the deep waters,
laid its foundations in the ocean's depths.

B: Who has the right to climb Yahweh's mountain?
Or stand in this holy place?

A: Those who are pure in act and in thought,
who do not worship idols
or make false promises.

B: Yahweh will bless them.
God their Saviour will give them salvation.

A: Such are the people who come to God,
who come into the presence of our God.

B: Fling wide the gates,
open the ancient doors,
and the Holy One will come in!

A: Who is this Holy One?
Yahweh, strong and mighty,
Yahweh, victorious in battle!

B: Fling wide the gates,
open the ancient doors,
and the Holy One will come in!

A: Who is this Holy One?
Yahweh, the glorious.

ALL: AMEN.

Psalm 27

A: God, you are my light and my salvation;
whom shall I fear?
You are the stronghold of my life;
of whom shall I be afraid?

B: When evildoers assail me,
uttering slanders against me,
my adversaries and foes,
they shall stumble and fall.

A: Though a host encamp against me,
my heart will not fear;
though war arise against me,
yet I will be confident.

B: One thing have I asked of you, Yahweh, this I seek:
to dwell in your house
all the days of my life,
to behold your beauty
and to contemplate on your Temple.

A: For you will hide me in your shelter
in the day of trouble,
you will conceal me under the cover of your tent
and will set me high upon a rock.

B: Though my father and my mother forsake me,
you will still accept me.

A: Teach me your way, O God,
and lead me on a level path
because of my enemies.

B: Give me not up to the will of my foes,
for false witnesses have risen against me,
and they breathe out violence.

A: I believe that I shall see the goodness of Yahweh
in the land of the living!

B: Wait for Yahweh;
be strong, and let your heart take courage.
Yes, wait for God!

ALL: AMEN.

Psalm 29

A: Give to Yahweh, O heavenly beings,
give to Yahweh glory and strength.

B: Give to Yahweh the glory of God's name;
worship Yahweh in holy array.

A: The voice of Yahweh is upon the waters;
the God of glory thunders upon many waters.

B: The voice of God is powerful;
the voice of Yahweh is full of majesty.

A: The voice of Yahweh breaks the cedars,
breaks the cedars of Lebanon,

B: Making Lebanon skip like a calf
and Sirion like a young wild ox.

A: The voice of Yahweh flashes forth flames of fire.

B: The voice of God shakes the wilderness,
the wilderness of Kadesh.

A: The voice of Yahweh makes the oaks twist
and strips the forests bare;
and in God's Temple all cry, "Glory"

B: Yahweh sits enthroned over the flood;
God sits enthroned forever.

ALL: MAY YAHWEH GIVE STRENGTH TO THE PEOPLE,
BLESSING THE PEOPLE WITH PEACE!
AMEN.

Psalm 33

ALL: SING OUT YOUR JOY TO THE CREATOR, GOOD PEOPLE;
FOR PRAISE IS FITTING FOR LOYAL HEARTS.

A: Give thanks to the Creator upon the harp,
with a ten-stringed lute sing songs.

B: O sing a new song;
play skillfully and loudly so all may hear.

A: For the word of the Creator is faithful,
and all God's works are to be trusted.

B: The Creator loves justice and right
and fills the earth with faithful love.

A: By the Creator's word the heavens were made,
by the breath of God's mouth all the stars.

B: The Creator collects the waves of the ocean
and gathers up the depths of the sea.

A: Let all the earth fear the Creator,
all who live in the world honour God.

B: The Creator spoke and it came to be;
commanded, it sprang into existence.

A: The Creator frustrates the plans of the nations,
overthrows the designs of the peoples.

B: The Creator's own designs shall last forever,
the plans of God's heart for all ages.

A: They are happy whose God is the Creator,
the people God has chosen.

B: From the heavens the Creator looks out,
and sees all the children of the earth.

A: A ruler is not protected by an army,
nor a warrior preserved by strength.

B: It is vain to hope for safety in a horse;
despite its power it cannot save.

A: The Creator looks on those who stand in reverence,
on those who hope in God's love −

B: To rescue their souls from death,
to keep them alive in famine.

A: Our soul is waiting for God,
our help and our shield.

B: In the Creator our hearts find joy.
We trust in God's holy name.

ALL: MAY YOUR FAITHFUL LOVE BE UPON US, O GOD,
AS WE PLACE ALL OUR HOPE IN YOU.
AMEN.

Psalm 40

A: I waited and waited for you, Yahweh!
Now at last you have turned to me
and heard my cry for help.

B: You have lifted me out of the horrible pit,
out of the mud of the marsh;
you set my feet on a rock
and steadied my steps.

A: Yahweh, you have put a new song in my mouth —
a song of praise.
Many will look on in awe
and will put their trust in you.

B: Happy are those who put their trust in Yahweh
and do not side with rebels who stray after false gods.

A: How many wonders you have done for us,
Yahweh, our God!
How many plans you have made for us,
You have no equal.
I want to proclaim your deeds again and again,
but they are more than I can count.

B: You, who wanted no sacrifice or oblation,
opened my ear;
you asked no holocaust or sacrifice for sin.

A: Then I said, "Here I am! I have come!"

B: In the scroll of the book it is prescribed for me
to obey your will.
My God, I have always loved your Law
from the depths of my being.

A: I have always proclaimed the justice of Yahweh
in the Great Assembly;
nor do I mean to stop proclaiming,
as you know well.

B: I have never kept your justice hidden within myself,
but have spoken of your faithfulness and saving help;
I have made no secret of your love and faithfulness
in the Great Assembly.

A: For your part, Yahweh,
do not withold your mercy from me!
May your love and faithfulness constantly protect me.

ALL: AMEN.

Psalm 42

A: Like the deer that yearns
for running streams,
so my soul is yearning
for you, my God.

B: My soul is thirsting for God, the living God.
When can I enter to see the face of God?

A: My tears have become my food night and day,
and I hear it said all day long:
"Where is your God?"

B: I will remember all these things
as I pour out my soul:
how I would lead the joyous procession
into the house of God,
with cries of gladness and thanksgiving,
the multitude wildly happy.

A: Why are you so sad, my soul?
Why sigh within me?
Hope in God;
for I will yet praise my saviour and my God.

B: My soul is downcast within me
when I think of you,
from the land of Jordan and Mount Hermon,
from the Hill of Mizar.

A: Deep is calling on deep
as the waterfalls roar:
your breakers and all your waves
crashed over me.

B: By day Yahweh will send loving-kindness;
by night I will sing praise to the God of my life.

A: I will say to God, my rock:
"Why have you forgotten me?
Why do I go mourning,
oppressed by the foe?"

B: With cries that pierce me to the heart,
my enemies revile me,
saying to me all day:
"Where is your God?"

A: Why are you oppressed, my soul —
why cry within me?
Hope in God; I will praise Yahweh,
my saviour and my God.

ALL: AMEN.

Psalm 46

ALL: GOD IS OUR REFUGE AND STRENGTH,
OUR EVER-PRESENT HELP IN DISTRESS.

A: Though the earth trembles,
and mountains slide into the sea,
we have no fear.

B: Waters foam and roar,
and mountains shake at their surging;
but the God of hosts is with us —
our stronghold, the God of the faithful people.

A: There is a river
whose streams give joy to the city of God,
the holy dwelling of the Most High.

B: God is in its midst; it stands firm.
God will aid it at the break of day.

A: Even if nations are in chaos, and kingdoms fall,
God's voice resounds; the earth melts away.

B: Yahweh is with us;
the God of the faithful people is our stronghold.

A: Come! See the deeds of the Most High,
the marvellous things God has done on earth;

B: All over the world, God has stopped wars —
breaking bows, splintering spears,
burning the shields with fire.

A: "Be still! and know that I am God,
exalted among the nations, exalted upon the earth."

ALL: THE MOST HIGH IS WITH US;
OUR STRONGHOLD IS THE GOD OF THE FAITHFUL PEOPLE.
AMEN.

Psalm 72

ALL: O GOD, WITH YOUR JUDGEMENT AND WITH YOUR JUSTICE,
ENDOW THE LEADERS.

A: They shall govern your people with justice
and your afflicted ones with righteousness.

B: The mountains will bring peace for the people,
and the hills justice.

A: They shall defend the afflicted among the people,
save the children of the poor,
and crush the oppressor.

B: May they endure as long as the sun
and like the moon through all generations.

A: They shall be like rain coming down on the field,
like showers watering the earth.

B: Virtue shall flower in their days,
and world peace till the moon is no more.

A: May they rule from sea to sea,
and from the river to the ends of the earth.

B: For they shall rescue the poor when they cry out
and the afflicted when they have no one to help them.

A: They shall have pity for the needy and the poor;
they shall save the lives of the poor.

B: From oppression and violence they shall redeem them,
and precious shall their blood be.

A: To them, long life and continuous prayers;
day by day shall they be blessed.

B: May grain be in abundance on the earth,
and on the tops of the mountains
the crops shall rustle like Lebanon.
The city dwellers shall flourish like the grass of the fields.

A: Blessed be their name forever;
their name shall remain as long as the sun.
In them shall all the nations of the earth be blessed;
all the nations shall proclaim their happiness.

B: Blessed be Yahweh, the God of the faithful people,
who alone does wondrous deeds.

ALL: AND BLESSED FOREVER BE GOD'S GLORIOUS NAME;
MAY THE WHOLE EARTH BE FILLED WITH GOD'S GLORY.
AMEN.

Psalm 82

A: God arises in the divine assembly
and judges in the midst of the gods:

B: "How long will you defend the unjust
and favour the cause of the wicked?"

A: Defend the poor and the orphaned;
render justice to the afflicted and the oppressed.

B: Rescue the lowly and the poor;
from the clutches of the wicked deliver them.

A: They have neither knowledge nor understanding —
they walk about blindly.
All the order of the world is shaken.

B: I said: "You are gods,
all of you.

A: Yet like mortals you shall die —
fall like any ruler."

ALL: RISE, O GOD; JUDGE THE EARTH,
FOR YOURS ARE ALL THE NATIONS.   AMEN.

Psalm 93

ALL: O GOD, YOU REIGN; YOU ARE ROBED IN SPLENDOUR
AND CLOTHED WITH STRENGTH.
THE WORLD IS FIRMLY ESTABLISHED; IT CANNOT BE MOVED.

A: Your throne has stood since long ago;
you are everlasting.

B: The seas have lifted up, O Yahweh,
the seas have lifted up their voice;
the seas have lifted up their pounding waves.

A: More powerful than the thunder of the great waters,
mightier than the breakers of the sea —
Yahweh is powerful on high.

B: Your decrees stand firm;
holiness adorns your house
for endless days.

ALL: AMEN.

Psalm 96

ALL: SING YAHWEH A NEW SONG!
SING TO YAHWEH, YOU LANDS!

A: Sing to Yahweh; bless God's name.
Proclaim God's salvation day after day.

B: Tell God's glory among the nations;
tell God's wondrous deeds to all people.

A: For Yahweh is great; loud must be God's praise.
Yahweh is to be feared above all Gods.

B: All the gods of the nations are as nothing.
Yahweh created the heavens;

A: Splendour and majesty are in God's presence,
power and beauty in God's sanctuary.

B: Families of the nations give all honour to Yahweh,
give glory and praise to God.

A: Bring gifts; bear them before God.

B: Worship Yahweh in the sacred court;
tremble before Yahweh, all the earth!

A: Say among the nations, "Yahweh is our Rock!"
Yahweh has made the world unshakeable;
Yahweh will judge each nation with equity.

B: Let the heavens be glad, and the earth rejoice;
let the sea and all that it holds resound.

A: Let the fields and all that is in them exult;
let all the forests cry out for joy

B: at the presence of Yahweh, for God comes to judge the earth,
to judge the world with justice and the nations with truth.

ALL: AMEN.

Psalm 98

ALL: SING A NEW SONG TO YAHWEH,
WHO HAS DONE WONDERFUL DEEDS,
WHOSE RIGHT HAND AND WHOSE HOLY ARM
HAVE BROUGHT SALVATION.

A: Yahweh has made salvation known,
has shown justice to the nations,

B: And has remembered the house of the faithful
in truth and love.
All the ends of the earth have seen
the saving power of our God.

A: Sing praise to Yahweh all the earth;
ring out your joy.

B: Sing psalms to Yahweh with the harp,
with the sound of music.

A: With trumpets and the sound of the horn,
acclaim Yahweh.

B: Let the sea and all within it resound,
the world and all its peoples.

A: Let the rivers clap their hands
and the mountains ring out their joy

B: at the presence of the Just Judge who comes,
who comes to rule the earth.
Yahweh will rule the world with justice
and the peoples with fairness.

ALL: AMEN.

Psalm 100

ALL: SHOUT FOR JOY TO GOD,
ALL THE LANDS!

A: Serve God with gladness!
Come into God's presence with joyful singing!

B: Know that Yahweh is God!
Yahweh made us, and we belong to God;
we are God's people and the sheep of God's pasture.

A: Enter God's gates with thanksgiving
and the courts with praise!
Give thanks to God; bless God's name!

B: For Yahweh is good;
God's steadfast love endures forever,
and God's faithfulness to all generations.

ALL: AMEN.

Psalm 103

A: Bless Yahweh, O my soul.
Bless God's holy name, all that is in me!

B: Bless Yahweh, O my soul,
and remember God's faithfulness:

A: In forgiving all your offences,
in healing all your diseases,

B: In redeeming your life from destruction,
in crowning you with love and compassion,

A: In filling your years with good things,
in renewing your youth like an eagle's.

B: Yahweh does justice
and always takes the side of the oppressed.

A: God's ways were revealed to Moses,
and Yahweh's deeds to the faithful nation.

B: Yahweh is merciful and forgiving,
slow to anger, rich in love;

A: Yahweh's wrath does not last forever;
it exists a short time only.

B: We are never threatened, never punished
as our guilt and our sins deserve.

A: As the height of heaven over earth
is the greatness of Yahweh's faithful love
for those who fear God.

B: Yahweh takes our sins away
farther than the east is from the west.

A: As tenderly as parents treat their children,
so Yahweh has compassion on those who fear God.

B: Yahweh knows what we are made of;
Yahweh remembers that we are dust.

A: The human lasts no longer than grass,
lives no longer than a flower in the field.

B: One gust of wind, and that one is gone,
never to be seen there again.

A: But Yahweh's faithful love for those who fear God
lasts from all eternity and forever,
so too God's justice to their children's children,

B: As long as they keep the covenant
and remember to obey its precepts.

A: Yahweh has established a throne in the heavens
and rules over all.

B: Bless Yahweh, all angels, mighty in strength
to enforce God's word, attentive to every command.

A:	Bless Yahweh, all nations, servants who do God's will.
B:	Bless Yahweh, all creatures in every part of the world. Bless Yahweh, O my soul.
ALL:	AMEN.

Psalm 113

ALL:	ALLELUIA! PRAISE, YOU SERVANTS OF YAHWEH, PRAISE THE NAME OF YAHWEH!
A:	May Yahweh's name be blessed both now and forever!
B:	From east to west, from north to south, praised be the name of Yahweh!
A:	High above all nations, Yahweh! Your glory transcends the heavens!
B:	Who is like you, Yahweh our God? Enthroned so high, you have to stoop
A:	To see the heavens and earth!
B:	You raise the poor from the dust and lift the needy from the dunghill
A:	To give them a place with rulers, with the nobles of your people.
B:	Yahweh, you give the barren a home, making them glad with children.
ALL:	AMEN.

Psalm 116

A:	I love you, Yahweh, because you have heard my voice and my supplications,
B:	Because you have inclined your ear to me. Therefore I will call on you as long as I live.
A:	The cords of death encompassed me; the pangs of Sheol laid hold on me; I suffered sorrow and anguish.
B:	Then I called on your name, Yahweh: "Oh Yahweh, I beseech you, save my life!"
A:	Gracious are you, Yahweh, and righteous; you are full of compassion.
B:	You protect the simplehearted; when I was brought low, you saved me.
A:	Be at rest once more, O my soul, for Yahweh has been good to you.

B: For you, Yahweh, have delivered my soul from death,
my eyes from tears,
my feet from stumbling.

A: I walk before you, Yahweh,
in the land of the living.

B: I believe even when I say,
"I am completely crushed."

A: In my dismay I declared,
"No one can be relied on."

B: What return can I make to you, Yahweh
for all your goodness to me?

A: I will take up the cup of salvation,
invoking your name.

B: I will fulfill what I vowed to you
in the presence of all the people.

ALL: AMEN.

Psalm 121

A: I lift my eyes to the mountains.
Where is help to come from?

B: My help comes from Yahweh,
who made heaven and earth.

A: Yahweh does not let our footsteps slip!
Our guard does not sleep!

B: The guardian of the faithful people
does not slumber or sleep.

A: Yahweh guards you, shades you.
With Yahweh at your right hand

B: The sun cannot harm you by day
nor the moon at night.

A: Yahweh guards you from harm,
protects your lives;

B: Yahweh watches over your coming and going,
now and for always.

ALL: AMEN.

Psalm 126

A: When God brought back the captives of Zion,
we were like those who dream.

B: Then our mouths were filled with laughter
and our tongues with rejoicing;
then they said among the nations,
"Yahweh has done great things for them."

A:	Yahweh has done great things for us; we are truly glad.
B:	Restore our fortunes, Yahweh, like the streams in the Negeb!
A:	May those who sow in tears reap with songs of joy!
B:	Those that go forth weeping, carrying the seed for sowing, shall come home with shouts of joy, bringing the sheaves with them.
ALL:	AMEN.

Psalm 130

A:	Out of the depths I cry to you, O God. Hear my voice!
B:	Let your ears be attentive to my cry for mercy.
A:	If you, O God, mark our guilt, who can stand?
B:	But with you is forgiveness; and for this we revere you.
A:	I trust in you, O God, my soul trusts in your word.
B:	My soul waits for you, O God. More than sentinels wait for the dawn, let your people wait for you.
A:	For with you is faithful and plentiful redemption.
B:	You will redeem your people from all their iniquities.
ALL:	AMEN.

Psalm 133

ALL:	HOW GOOD IT IS, HOW PLEASANT, FOR GOD'S PEOPLE TO LIVE IN UNITY.
A:	It is like the precious oil running down from Aaron's head and beard, down to the collar of his robes.
B:	It is like the dew on Mount Hermon falling on the hills of Zion. For there Yahweh has promised a blessing, life that never ends.
ALL:	AMEN.

Psalm 138

A: I thank you, Yahweh, with all my heart;
      I sing praise to you before the angels.

B: I worship at your holy temple and praise your name
      because of your constant love and faithfulness,
      because you have shown that you and your word are exalted.

A: You answered me when I called to you;
      you built up strength within me.

B: All the rulers of the earth will praise you, Yahweh,
      because they have heard your promises.

A: They will sing about your ways
      and about your great glory.

B.   Even though you are exalted,
      you care for the lowly.
      The proud cannot hide from you.

A: Even when I am surrounded by troubles,
      you keep me safe;
      you oppose my angry enemies and save me by your power.

B: You will do everything you have promised me;
      Yahweh, your faithful love endures forever.
      Complete the work that you have begun.

ALL: AMEN.

Psalm 139

A: Yahweh, you search me and know me.

B: You know if I am standing or sitting
      You perceive my thoughts from far away.

A: Whether I walk or lie down, you are watching;
      you are familiar with all my ways.

B: Before a word is even on my tongue, Yahweh,
      you know it completely.

A: Close behind and close in front you hem me in,
      shielding me with your hand.

B: Such knowledge is beyond my understanding,
      too high beyond my reach.

A: Where could I go to escape your spirit?
      Where could I flee from your presence?

B: If I climb to the heavens, you are there;
      there, too, if I sink to Sheol.

A: If I flew to the point of sunrise —
      or far across the sea —

B: Your hand would still be guiding me,
      your right hand holding me.

A: If I asked darkness to cover me
and light to become night around me,

B: That darkness would not be dark to you;
night would shine as the day.

A: You created my inmost being
and knit me together in my mother's womb.

B: For all these mysteries —
for the wonder of myself,
for the wonder of your works —
I thank you.

A: You know me through and through
from having watched my bones take shape
when I was being formed in secret,
woven together in the womb.

B: You have seen my every action;
all were recorded in your book —
my days determined
even before the first one began.

A: God, your thoughts are mysterious!
How vast is their sum.

B: I could no more count them than I could count the sand!
And even if I could, you would still be with me.

A: God, search me and know my heart;
probe me and know my thoughts.

B: Make sure I do not follow evil ways,
and guide me in the way of life eternal.

ALL: AMEN.

Psalm 142

A: With all my voice I cry to you, Yahweh;
with all my voice I entreat you.

B: I pour out my complaint before you;
I tell you all my distress.

A: When my spirit faints within me,
you, Yahweh, know my path.
On the way where I shall walk
they have hidden a snare to trap me.

B: I look on my right and see:
there is no one who takes my part.
I have lost all means of escape,
there is no one who cares for my life.

A: I cry to you, Yahweh,
I have said: "You are my refuge,
all I have in the land of the living."

B: Listen, then, to my cry,
      for I am in the depths of distress.
      Rescue me from those who pursue me,
      for they are too strong for me.

A: Bring my soul out of this prison,
      and then I shall praise your name.
      Around me the just will gather
      because of your goodness to me.

ALL: AMEN.

Psalm 146

A: Alleluia!
      Praise Yahweh, O my soul!

B: I will praise you, Yahweh, all my life;
      I will sing praise to you as long as I live.

A: Do not put your trust in rulers,
      in humans in whom there is no salvation.

B: When their spirits depart they return to the earth;
      on that very day their plans perish.

A: Happy those whose help is the God of Jacob and Rachel,
      whose hope is in Yahweh, their God,

B: The Maker of heaven and earth,
      the sea, and all that is in them;

A: Who keeps faith forever,
      secures justice for the oppressed,
      and gives food to the hungry.

B: Yahweh, you set captives free
      and give sight to the blind.
      You raise up those that were bowed down
      and love the just.

A: You protect strangers;
      the orphan and the widow you sustain,
      but the way of the wicked you thwart.

ALL: YAHWEH SHALL REIGN FOREVER,
      THROUGH ALL GENERATIONS.
      ALLELUIA.
      AMEN.

Psalm 148

ALL: PRAISE GOD FROM THE HEAVENS;
PRAISE GOD IN THE HEIGHTS;

A: Praise God, all you angels;
praise God, all you heavenly hosts.

B: Praise God, sun and moon;
praise God, all you shining stars.

A: Praise God, you highest heavens,
and you waters above the heavens.

B: Let them praise the name of God,
who commanded and they were created.

A: God established them forever and ever
and gave a decree which shall not pass away.

B: Praise God all the earth,
you sea monsters and all depths,

A: Fire and hail, snow and mist,
storm winds that fulfill God's word.

B: You mountains and all you hills,
you fruit trees and all you cedars,

A: You wild beasts and all tame animals,
you creeping things and flying birds.

B: Let the rulers of the earth and all peoples
and all the judges of the earth −

A: Young men too, and maidens,
old women and men −

B: Praise the name of God
whose name alone is exalted;
whose majesty is above earth and heaven,
and who has raised the fortunes of the people.

ALL: GOD BE PRAISED BY ALL THE FAITHFUL ONES,
BY THE PEOPLE CLOSE TO GOD.
ALLELUIA.
AMEN.

INDEX

Appendix of General Worship Resources:

ACKNOWLEDGEMENTS

The Iona Community gratefully acknowledges the permission granted to use the following items included in the book which are copyright as described below. The Iona Community has attempted to contact the owners of all material which is copyright. We would be glad to have any omissions brought to our attention.

The hymn *Tell Out My Soul The Greatness Of The Lord* (based on the Magnificat, NEB) is written by the Rt. Rev. Timothy Dudley-Smith.

The hymn *Christ Is Alive* by Brian Wren is published by the Oxford University Press.

The psalms in the appendix are reprinted from *Psalms Anew: In Inclusive Language*, compiled by Nancy Schreck and Maureen Leach. (Winona, Minnesota, U.S.A.: Saint Mary's Press, 1986). Used by permission of the publisher. All rights reserved.

All the other material is either traditional or original to the Iona Community, to which application **must** be made in the first instance if it is desired that such material be reproduced commercially.

Apply to:
>The Copyright Manager, Wild Goose Publications,
>Pearce Institute, 840 Govan Road, Glasgow G51 3UU

OTHER PUBLICATIONS

The Iona Community has an increasing range of worship materials, which are complimentary to this volume. These include 3 volumes of *Wild Goose Songs*, Two volumes of *World Church Songs*, 9 books of scripts for use in worship or discussion, six cassettes of words and music, and a range of other books.

For a catalogue and further details apply to:
>The Sales Manager,
>Wild Goose Publications, The Iona Community,
>Pearce Institute, 840 Govan Road, Glasgow G51 3UU.
>Tel. 041 445 4561   Fax. 041 445 4295

®TM